Xanda & AP
maio /008

S0-AWK-290

PRAGUE
ENCOUNTER

SARAH JOHNSTONE

Prague Encounter

Published by Lonely Planet Publications Pty Ltd
ABN 36 005 607 983

Australia	Head Office, Locked Bag 1, Footscray, Vic 3011
	☎ 03 8379 8000 fax 03 8379 8111
	talk2us@lonelyplanet.com.au
USA	150 Linden St, Oakland, CA 94607
	☎ 510 893 8555
	toll free 800 275 8555
	fax 510 893 8572
	info@lonelyplanet.com
UK	72–82 Rosebery Avenue, Clerkenwell, London EC1R 4RW
	☎ 020 7841 9000 fax 020 7841 9001
	go@lonelyplanet.co.uk

This title was commissioned in Lonely Planet's London office and produced by: **Commissioning Editors** Janine Eberle, Korina Miller **Coordinating Editor** Andrea Dobbin **Coordinating Cartographer** Hunor Csutoros **Layout Designer** Jacqui Saunders **Assisting Editor** Kate Cody **Assisting Cartographers** Csanad Csutoros, Jacqueline Nguyen, Anita Banh, Daniel Fennessy, Joshua Geoghegan **Managing Editor** Bruce Evans **Managing Cartographers** Mark Griffiths, Malisa Plesa **Cover Designer** James Hardy **Project Manager** Fabrice Rocher **Series Designers** Nic Lehman, Wendy Wright **Language Content Coordinator** Quentin Frayne **Thanks to** Celia Wood, Sally Darmody, Laura Jane, Wayne Murphy, Paul Piaia, Lyahna Spencer

Our Readers Many thanks to the travellers who wrote to us with helpful hints, useful advice and interesting anecdotes. Stephen Addison, David Burnett, Simon Cliff, Jane de Raeve, Greg Fisher, Anna Fox, Jonathan Franklin, Karen Goodwin, Destin Singleton, Alan Walmsley, Debbie Xenophou

All images are copyright of the photographers unless otherwise indicated. Many of the images in this guide are available for licensing from **Lonely Planet Images:** www.lonelyplanetimages.com.

ISBN 978 1 74104 312 9

Printed through Colorcraft Ltd, Hong Kong.
Printed in China

HOW TO USE THIS BOOK
Colour-Coding & Maps

Colour-coding is used for symbols on maps and in the text that they relate to (eg all eating venues on the maps and in the text are given a green fork symbol). Each neighbourhood also gets its own colour, and this is used down the edge of the page and throughout that neighbourhood section.

Shaded yellow areas on the maps denote 'areas of interest' – for their historical significance, their attractive architecture or their great bars and restaurants. We encourage you to head to these areas and just start exploring!

Send us your feedback We love to hear from readers – your comments help make our books better. We read every word you send us, and we always guarantee that your feedback goes straight to the appropriate authors. The most useful submissions are rewarded with a free book. To send us your updates and find out about Lonely Planet events, newsletters and travel news visit our award-winning website: *lonelyplanet.com/contact*.

Note: We may edit, reproduce and incorporate your comments in Lonely Planet products such as guidebooks, websites and digital products, so let us know if you don't want your comments reproduced or your name acknowledged. For a copy of our privacy policy visit *lonelyplanet.com/privacy*.

SARAH JOHNSTONE

One of Sarah Johnstone's earliest Prague memories is a maître d' in an empty restaurant telling her group there was no table 'because we're full'. Being the perverse type, she was hooked. And although this beguiling, beautiful-looking city is now somewhat friendlier and has consolidated its position as one of Europe's top destinations, she's returned regularly. That's especially so since good friends relocated here in 2000. Born in Queensland, at home in London, Sarah makes her living as a freelance journalist. Having previously worked in environments ranging from business travel magazines to Reuters, she's just clocked up something like her 16th Lonely Planet book since 2002 (although, to tell the truth, she's losing count).

SARAH'S THANKS

Thanks to Dr Jana Stejskalová for rescuing me. Aleksander, Lindsay, Marusá, Luka and Miriam for moral support, translation, postbox, cake, wine and much more. Also Jaroslava Nováková, Marketá Chaloupková, John Allison, Dave Faries, Janek Jaros, Viki aka Nush Imogen, Irena Markovic, František Richter, Noah Lucas, Ivan Karhan, Jonathan, and Paul at Saints. Finally to my lovely Smíchov flatmates – Lorenzo (nightlife guru and master of pasta), Naomi (camera-wielding scourge of crypto-zoologists and fellow *cukrkáva* fiend) and Batiste (*philosphe* and inveterate mirror-borrower). Elmar, Lily and all that crew, too.

THE PHOTOGRAPHER

Doug Mckinlay has been a photographer for 20 years, having started out as a stringer in exotic war-zone locales from Cambodia to El Salvador. His travel and news images have appeared in publications such as the *Times*, the *Independent*, the *Guardian*, the *Mail*, *Conde Nast Traveller*, *Maxim*, the *Observer*, *High Life*, *CNN Traveller* and Lonely Planet guidebooks.

Cover photograph View of St Vitus Cathedral from Seifertova, Žižkov, Sean Gallup/Getty Images **Internal photographs** p83, p114, p129, p136 by Sarah Johnstone; p4, p12 Sean Gallup/Getty Images; p6, p32, p35, p36 Scott Barbour/Getty Images; p25, p30 CzechTourism; p26, p28 Prague Information Service. All other photographs by Lonely Planet Images, and by Doug Mckinlay except p48 Tim Hughes; p116, p149 Richard Nebesky.

Swing by the graceful Dancing Building (p97)

CONTENTS

THIS IS PRAGUE

Shock news: Prague is the new Prague. Or at least, like its sartorial equivalent, black, the Czech capital never goes out of fashion. The architectural embodiment of a thousand fairy-tale fantasies, this is a classic European city that – metaphorically and literally – it's time to revisit.

Nearly 20 years after the Velvet Revolution drew back the curtain on this intoxicating maze of winding cobblestone alleyways, the outside world thinks it knows Prague pretty well. It's drunk the peerless beer, read a little Kundera and Klíma, and crossed Charles Bridge. But besides Prague Castle, the Old Jewish Cemetery and the chiming Astronomical Clock, how much is understood about the original Kafkaesque town, really?

If you're looking for love at first sight, pint-sized Prague will deliver. (And if you want a reasonably priced booze-fuelled time, it'll provide that too.) However, the 'city of 100 spires' has other, unsung sides. Prague boasts Gothic, baroque and Art Nouveau architecture, but it's also the only place on earth with cubist furniture and buildings. A former Habsburg city, it's not just about free-flowing beer in traditional pubs, but also about ornate coffeehouses, and bars selling sweet Becherovka as well as bitter absinth.

In the district of Vinohrady stands an impressive 1930s church – the Most Sacred Heart – that modernists find as aesthetically pleasing as the castle's spiky St Vitus Cathedral. Just around the corner, the 1980s TV tower has sculptures of giant, blank-faced babies crawling up it. Even the city's famous castle has a matching chess piece in the citadel of Vyšehrad.

As rowdy stag parties slowly start drifting away to much-vaunted 'new Pragues' like Kraków and Riga, the mood in the original Prague seems slightly easier. The fact that the Czech capital is sprucing up some major landmarks and even pondering some cutting-edge architecture in central Letná Gardens provides yet another reason to consider it anew.

Top left Musician performing on Charles Bridge (p56) **Top right** Museum posters **Bottom** Eating out in Prague

>HIGHLIGHTS

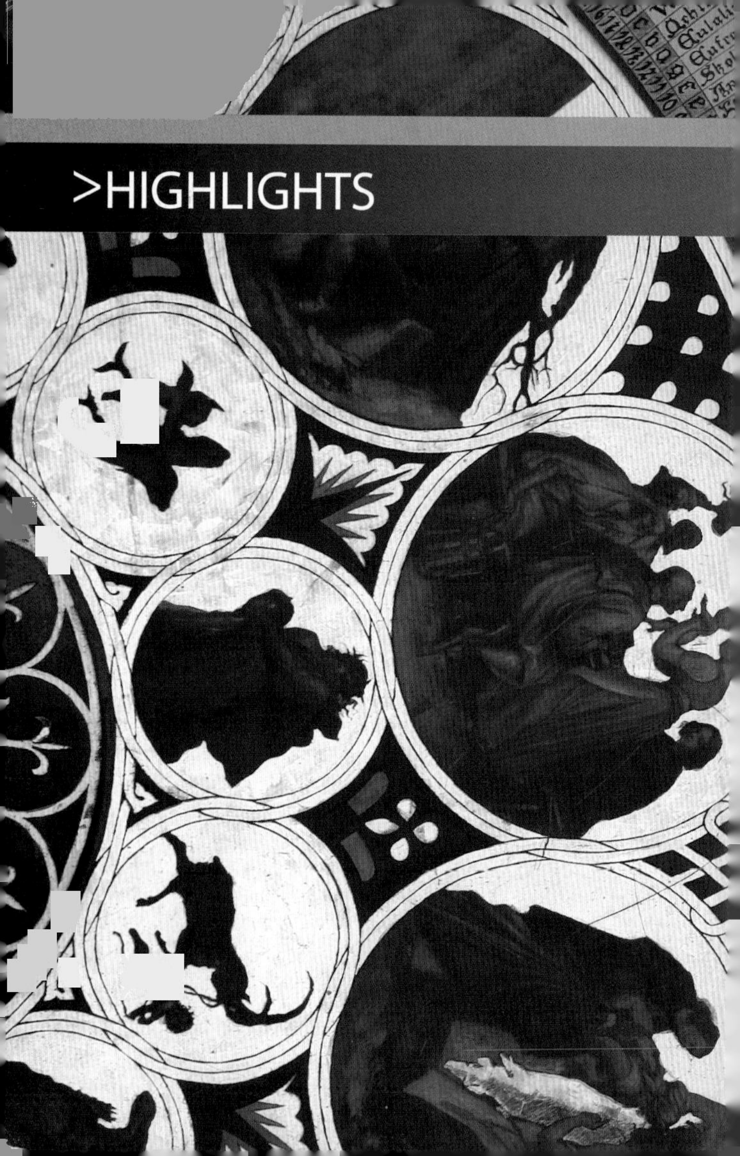

Astronomical Clock (p14)

>1 PRAGUE CASTLE

HIT THE LOFTY HEIGHTS OF PRAGUE CASTLE

Of all the sights in enchanting Prague, its castle contributes most to its picture-book appearance. Looming high above the Vltava's left bank – with the spires of the central St Vitus Cathedral piercing the sky and its long outer wall angled away from the river – this outrageously outsized fortress conjures up childhood fairy tales of a good king watching benevolently over his people.

Founded by Czech 'Přemysl' princes in the 9th century (see p166), Pražský hrad is still the official presidential residence. As the largest castle complex in the world, bigger than seven football fields, it thoroughly dominates this city of 1.2 million. Indeed, it's a national symbol.

Yet despite its huge size, the castle is relatively easy to 'do'. The Gothic-looking St Vitus Cathedral, with its viewing tower, beautiful stained-glass windows and ornate chapels, is pivotal. The tiny, 16th-century Golden Lane is still sweet, despite blatant tourist-ification; the gardens are gorgeous in summer; and the views from the old castle steps are always unmissable (particularly of an evening).

Elsewhere in the complex is the Story of Prague Castle, one of the slickest exhibitions in town, while the Toy Museum, with its entire floor of Barbie dolls, adds quirky appeal. The other churches, palaces and picture galleries here are even more a matter of personal taste. See p47 for further details on visiting.

>2 MALÁ STRANA
EXPLORE MALÁ STRANA'S WINDING STREETS OF AN EVENING

Winding your way over cobblestones under the gentle glow of old-fashioned street lamps, passing residents out walking their dachshunds – you'll find Malá Strana on an evening stroll all you imagined Prague to be. The Czech Republic might now be a proud EU member, but after the crowds of day-trippers have gone home the capital's so-called 'Lesser Quarter' can still feel quintessentially Central European.

Although there's plenty to see here before sunset (see p56), in the early evening you needn't set off anywhere particular. The beauty of the exercise is just to wander past baroque houses and down back lanes.

Up Tržiště and Vlašská are some interesting corners, as well as north of Charles Bridge around Mišenská. Approaching lovely Kampa Island (p57) from any direction – north, west or south – feels quite thrilling. Wander through the southern park here and gaze across the water at the golden-roofed National Theatre (p116) and nearby terraces, all lit up like a Christmas tree.

>3 CHARLES BRIDGE

BEAT THE CROWDS WITH A DAWN STROLL ACROSS CHARLES BRIDGE

This stone bridge across the Vltava River is a victim of its own success. It's easy to see how it became so popular, as the most direct and attractive route between Prague Castle and Staré Město (the Old Town). However, the fact that it's now so crowded 9am to 5pm (at least) means a radical solution is needed.

So, do something unusual in this beery city – get up early to beat the traffic. Easier, stay up all night and come here on your way home. With the sun behind you as you cross from Staré Město, and light bouncing off the river, you'll understand what the Charles Bridge fuss was about in the first place. A second-best alternative is to cross in the evenings, when the castle twinkles.

The bridge was commissioned by Emperor Charles IV in 1357, but was only finished in 1400 and took his name in the 19th century. See p56 for details of planned renovations. The most famous of 30 statues lining the bridge is of St John of Nepomuk. Although poor St John himself was supposedly chucked off the bridge, legend has it that if you rub the bronze plaque beneath him you'll return to Prague.

>4 THE OLD JEWISH CEMETERY

MEANDER THROUGH THE JUMBLE OF LEANING HEADSTONES IN THE OLD JEWISH CEMETERY

With 12,000 gravestones and some 100,000 bodies packed into a space the size of maybe five suburban gardens, Prague's Old Jewish Cemetery is like no other on earth. With crumbling headstones leaning left and right – pushed up and out by the graves that lie in 12 layers underneath – it bizarrely resembles a mouthful of crooked teeth.

Dating from the 15th century and one of Europe's oldest Jewish burial grounds, this is part of the city's multisite Jewish Museum (p77), which also encompasses the Maisel Synagogue, Spanish Synagogue, Pinkas Synagogue, Klaus Synagogue and Ceremonial Hall. (To visit the cemetery, you need to buy a ticket to the entire museum.)

Dispersed across the area of Prague's cramped 13th-century walled ghetto, which became the un-walled Jewish quarter of Josefov from the mid-19th century, the museum purports to tell the history of Jews in Bohemia. Being split across several sites, however, the narrative feels disjointed, so it's better to focus on outstanding individual features.

The overcrowded cemetery tops that list, and features the prominent grave of Rabbi Löw, the creator of the mythical mud-man cum slave 'Golem' (see the boxed text, p78). Also worth seeing are the renovated Spanish Synagogue and the striking Pinkas Synagogue, now a Holocaust Memorial engraved with the names of 80,000 murdered Bohemian Jews.

>5 THE ASTRONOMICAL CLOCK

INDULGE IN A BIT OF TOURIST KITSCH WATCHING THE ASTRONOMICAL CLOCK CHIME

One of the world's best-known tourist attractions is also one of its leading 'is that it?' experiences. Every hour between 9am and 9pm, expectant crowds assemble before Prague's Old Town Hall to watch the Astronomical Clock (p71) do its thing by chiming.

Death rings a bell, inverts his hourglass, and the 12 apostles parade through the windows above the clock. Then, a cock crows. The noise sounds like someone blowing a raspberry. People laugh, slightly embarrassed. That's it really – in 45 seconds flat.

Yet despite this underwhelming performance, the clock remains a 'must-do' for most visitors and one of Prague's leading five sights. After all, it's photogenic, quick to tick off your list and an intriguing puzzle to decipher (see the boxed text, p74). Unless you set eyes on it, you may not feel you've really been to Prague, and it brings you to the Old Town Sq, the (alas frequently clogged) heart of the city.

The gothic spires of the Church of Our Lady Before Týn (p74) loom over the eastern perimeter; in the middle stands a statue of heroic Czech reformer Jan Hus – a kind of Martin Luther meets Joan of Arc (see p166). Reconstruction work means the statue will probably still be under wraps when you read this, but you can peek through the scaffolding.

>6 TRADITIONAL PUBS

SUP WORLD-BEATING CZECH BEER IN A TRADITIONAL PUB
Even teetotallers know Czechs brew some of the world's best beers.
So where better to sample these pale, golden lagers and rarer dark varieties than in the country where they're produced? In Prague's many traditional pubs, *pivo* (beer) is dirt-cheap. But the crowning glory, the extra drop in your tankard, is that your glass is often replenished without your asking – which makes the capital of Budvar, Gambrinus, Pilsner Urquell and Staropramen beer-heaven for many drinkers.

Indeed, Czech beer-drinking isn't just a pastime, it's a patriotic tradition. During the Austro-Hungarian Empire, when Vienna ruled Prague, the local *hospoda* (pub) or *pivnice* (beer hall) was one place local culture was sustained and nourished. Leading author Jaroslav Hašek wrote the *Good Soldier Schwejk* in pubs. In the 20th century, U Zlatého Tygra (p92) was a second home to writer Bohumil Hrabal (*I served the King of England*).

Though they often make delicious home-brews, fame has unfortunately stripped some Prague pubs of authenticity. The renowned U Fleků (p113) is full of non-Czechs and even outlets like U Medvídků (p91) and U Vejvodů (p91) can feel touristy.

But central U Rudolfina (p91) and U Černého Vola (pictured above; p53) retain a local air – sometimes by scowling at newcomers! – and there are other favourites under this guide's 'Drink' listings; see p152 for a quick rundown of Czech beer, pub etiquette and absinth.

>7 WENCESLAS SQUARE

REFLECT ON PAST PROTESTS AND REVOLUTION IN WENCESLAS SQUARE

Immortalised in postcards showing the equestrian statue of 'good king' Wenceslas (see the boxed text, p167) in front of the National Museum (p101), the surprisingly long and rectangular Wenceslas Sq (p103) was once a gathering point for proud Czechs, demonstrators and communist refuseniks.

Student Jan Palach burned himself to death near the National Museum in early 1969 to protest against the Soviet invasion after 1968's liberal 'Prague Spring'. Twenty years later the square became a focal point for the Velvet Revolution (see p144). On 24 November 1989, when deposed 'Prague Spring' president Alexander Dubček appeared beside prominent dissident and president-to-be Václav Havel on the balcony of the Melantrich Building (No 36), the crowd below knew Czechoslovak communism had reached its endgame.

Virtually untrammelled capitalism has reigned ever since, filling the square with British stag parties, persistent cabaret touts, greedy cabbies, bureaux de change and a soulless procession of second-rate cafés, fast-food outlets and *Bankrot* (clearance sale) shops.

Still, visiting the symbolic Wenceslas Statue (p105) is a good way to reconnect with the past, especially with the small memorials to communist victims near it.

For an iconoclast's amusing take on the post-communist era, finish your visit in the nearby Lucerna Passage (p100). Here artist David Černý (see also p23) has Wenceslas astride a dead horse.

>8 KAFKA'S PRAGUE

BE INSPIRED BY FRANZ KAFKA'S LITERARY GENIUS

'Someone must have been telling lies about Josef K, for without having done anything wrong, he was arrested one fine morning' – that opening line to Franz Kafka's *The Trial* (1925) is widely considered among the greatest in world literature. The words are also a testament to Prague's disorientating nature; and in the writer's home city it's hard not to be moved by his genius.

Of course, it's simple to pay tribute to Kafka by visiting his birthplace (p75) or grave (p120), and admiring the monument (p74) beside the Spanish Synagogue. However, fans can also delve more into the novelist's complex relationship with Prague, which he complained was small and claustrophobic but got under your skin.

The Franz Kafka Museum (p57) broaches this subject, but you also get a sense of what drove Kafka just going round in circles in Staré Město (see p142 for a more straightforward walking tour). In the Old Town's labyrinthine maze of alleyways and secret corners lies the metaphysical geography to his books. Don't forget to buy *The Trial* and read or re-read him.

>9 WALLENSTEIN GARDEN

LEAVE THE REAL WORLD BEHIND IN THE SECRETIVE WALLENSTEIN GARDEN

Prague has many tucked-away treasures but few as appealing as this formal Italian garden, hidden behind walls in a busy district. As you step from Malá Strana's streets into 1.7 hectares of manicured hedges, Greek gods, fish ponds, fountains and peacocks, it sometimes feels like you've gone through the looking glass, Alice-in-Wonderland style. This magical garden belongs to the baroque Wallenstein Palace, built in the 1620s and now home to the Czech Senate.

Experts usually give top billing to the garden's three-arch 'Sala Terrena' (pavilion), which is decorated with frescoes from Greek mythology. However, the immediately striking feature is the dripstone 'stalactite' wall at the western end. It artificially recreates a limestone cave or grotto, with many shapes – from animals to grotesque faces – in its uneven dark-grey surface.

The garden's bronze statues are copies, replacing originals stolen by invading Swedish soldiers in 1648. (Beside the Greek gods, look out for Satan being thrashed by a naked saint!) See p62 for opening times.

>10 WALK FROM PETŘÍN TO STRAHOV

CATCH SOME OF THE CITY'S BEST VIEWS BETWEEN PETŘÍN HILL AND STRAHOV MONASTERY

A dinky funicular railway (p59) rides up to Prague's best picnic spot – the 318m-high grassy knoll of Petřín Hill (p59), which is also popular with joggers, dog-walkers, lovers, families and wintertime tobogganists and skiers. From here you have magnificent vistas across the 'city of 100 spires', and the panorama gets better as you follow the trail down and around to Strahov Monastery (p46).

Loved by Victorian-era leisure-seekers, Petřín wouldn't be complete without its brace of fun-but-slightly-cheesy attractions. So there's a mirror maze (p60) and the Petřín Tower (p60), a mini-Eiffel replica built for the 1891 Prague Exposition. This was Prague's main telecoms transmitter, until replaced by the brutalist Žižkov TV Tower (p121) opposite. Riding up to Petřín you can alight en route at Restaurant Nebozízek (p67), and on the summit you'll also find an observatory (p62).

Ambling from Petřín to Strahov, you follow an arc above the city, until its bridges line up crossing the Vltava River. Follow the upper dirt path or climb the wooden steps from the paved lower path to the semicircular lookout point behind the monastery, where the view is one of the best in Prague.

At the monastery complex, the stunning Strahov Library and the quirky Miniatures Museum (p45) await. You can even continue to the castle from here.

>11 GRAND CAFÉS

WHILE AWAY AN HOUR IN AN ORNATE GRAND CAFÉ

Prague is known for pubs, Vienna for its coffeehouses. Yet the Czech capital also boasts grand cafés that rival their Austrian cousins in looks. True, the actual coffee is poorer and less varied, but the atmosphere is equivalent, and since the days of the Austro-Hungarian Empire onwards, Prague's ornate, high-ceilinged coffeehouses have acted as public meeting spaces, hotbeds of political subversion and literary salons.

At various times Franz Kafka, robot 'creator' Karel Čapek (p171) and Albert Einstein all drank at Café Louvre (p108), while across the road at Kavárna Slavia (p112) patrons included Milan Kundera, Václav Havel and other anticommunist dissidents.

But you don't need to be interested in following in your hero's footsteps; such grand cafés are simply wonderful places to rest your own feet. The café in the stunning Municipal House (pictured above; p90) is one of the most famous, but a few recently reopened cafés – the cubist Grand Café Orient (p90) and Café Savoy (p64) – will also do the trick. However, for residents' regular haunts, you're better off choosing the charming Café Louvre or the Art Nouveau Kavárna Lucerna (p112).

>12 MUNICIPAL HOUSE

ADMIRE THE ART NOUVEAU OPULENCE OF MUNICIPAL HOUSE

It's hard to get past its jaw-dropping looks, but this lavish wedding-cake of an Art Nouveau structure is one of Prague's most-visited landmarks *and* one of its most culturally significant buildings.

In the early 20th century, with Czechs seeking independence from the fading Austro-Hungarian Empire, some 30 leading artists and architects – including Alfons Mucha – poured their talents and national aspirations into it.

The architectural climax of the so-called Czech National Revival, Municipal House was completed in 1912. And the hard work was briefly rewarded when the first independent Czechoslovak Republic was declared in 1918 inside its concert hall. Sadly, the building then fell prey to decades of neglect. However, after a 1997 restoration it's back, with many ways to see it.

Some visitors just photograph the façade or visit the downstairs café (p90) and French restaurant. Others come for concerts under the Art Nouveau dome of Smetana Hall (p95). The city's biggest concert hall, with 1200 seats, this is where the first notes of the Prague Spring festival (see p27) are played every year.

Real fans, however, take a tour to learn about the building's extensive national symbolism and to see the octagonal Lord Mayor's Hall, with stained glass windows and everything else designed by Mucha. This tour also covers Smetana Hall; see p75 for more details.

>13 VYŠEHRAD

HEAD FOR A PICNIC ON VYŠEHRAD'S HIGH PLATEAU

Prague's second 'castle' is very different from its first but equally dramatic in its own right. Indeed, it's been centuries since any real castle stood here, amid the remains of the city's second historic settlement. Unlike Pražský hrad and its cluster of ancient buildings, Vyšehrad today is essentially a large, tall plateau bordered by vertiginous ramparts.

However, this ruined citadel more than atones for any architectural shortcomings with breathtaking views south of the Vltava River and north over Prague. Up here, you feel you're floating above the city.

Although Vyšehrad's grassy expanses make it perfect for a picnic, it does boast a few individual buildings. Among these is the 19th-century Church of SS Peter & Paul, whose interior presents a swirling acid trip of colourful Art Nouveau frescoes.

Next door is a mournful but beautiful cemetery, where some 600 Czech notables are buried. Painter Alfons Mucha, writers Jan Neruda and Karel Čapek and composers Antonín Dvořák and Bedřich Smetana all lie here – check the plan at the gate.

Otherwise, for the very few practical details you'll need when visiting Vyšehrad, turn to p104.

>14 ČERNÝ SCULPTURES

LAUGH YOUR HEAD OFF AT DAVID ČERNÝ'S CHEEKY PUBLIC SCULPTURES

Prague and cutting-edge modern art are hardly synonymous in the global imagination. Yet the quaint city on the Vltava harbours a series of pleasant surprises for those who enjoy wacky things.

Huge babies climbing the Žižkov TV Tower (p121), a Sigmund Freud lookalike dangling above a lane by his fingertips (p75) and two cybermen writing out famous literary quotes with their piss (p62) – these are just some of the sculptures bad-boy artist David Černý has planted among Prague's streets.

Černý (1967–) made international headlines in 1991 by painting a Soviet tank on a WWII memorial pink. Since then he's enjoyed overseas stints and busied himself at home – through his sculpture and public behaviour – enthusiastically outraging people.

In another major work Černý has 'good king' Wenceslas mounted on a dead, upside-down horse (pictured above; see p100). If your interest is piqued, you could also venture to see 'Quo Vadis' (p62) and 'Brown-nosing' (p61). For more on the artist himself, head to www.davidcerny.cz. Or read his, ahem, 'biography': *David Černý: The Fucking Years* (available at Žižkov Tower).

>15 CZECH CUBISM

GET A HANDLE ON QUIRKY CZECH CUBIST DESIGN

Pablo Picasso and Georges Braque practised it in painting and sculpture, but only the Czechs ever applied cubism to architecture and furniture. The result was chairs with spiders' legs, boxes shaped like crystals, angular ashtrays and buildings like folded origami pieces. Exploring these and other weird and wonderful artefacts from the period (1911–24) make a perfect rainy-day pursuit.

In fact, there aren't too many decent museums in Prague, but four of the best contain works from the cubist period. The Museum of Czech Cubism (pictured above; p76) gives a concentrated blast of pointy-angled couches and the like, while the stunning Veletržní Palace (p133) has half a floor devoted to similar. Cubist ceramics are on show and sale at the Museum of Decorative Arts (p76). And while the fantastically located Kampa Museum (p57) focuses more on contemporary art, it does have cubist sculptures and paintings from Czech artists Otto Gutfreund and František Kupka.

If the weather clears up, don't forget to pop around the corner from Wenceslas Sq to see the world's only cubist lamppost (p97).

>PRAGUE DIARY

From festivals of classical music to ancient pagan rituals, and from celebrations of Roma culture to a leading literary get-together, Prague has something extra to offer visitors all through the year. It's true that events thin out during the summer crush, when Prazaks head for the country and leave their city to the tourists. However, the spring and autumn calendars are particularly full. Most people know that traditional Easter and Christmas celebrations make these both excellent times to visit this quaint city. However, with ancient carnival traditions and an electronic music festival in February, there's even something interesting in Prague in the dead of winter.

Painted Easter eggs

JANUARY

Three Kings' Day (Svátek Tří králů)

Three Kings' Day marks the end of the Christmas season on 6 January; it's celebrated with carolling, bell ringing and gifts to the poor.

Anniversary of Jan Palach's Death

On 19 January people gather on Wenceslas Sq at the Jan Palach Memorial (p100) to remember the student who burned himself to death in 1969 in protest against the Soviet occupation.

FEBRUARY

Masopust

www.carnevale.cz (central Prague),
www.praha3.cz (Žižkov, Czech only)

Street parties, fireworks, concerts and revelry mark the Czech version of carnival (pictured left). Banned by the communists, this ancient tradition was first revived in Žižkov in 1993. Žižkov still parties hardest, although the rest of Prague is joining in. Celebrations start Friday and culminate in a masked parade on Shrove Tuesday.

St Matthew Fair (Matějská pouť)

From 24 February to Easter, Výstaviště (p133) is transformed into a funfair with rollercoasters, fairground rides, shooting galleries and myriad food stalls.

Sperm Festival

www.sperm.cz

This annual festival of electronic music incorporates avant-garde cinema and radio too. Previous years have opened at the Roxy (p94) and ended with concerts at Abaton (p137).

MARCH

Easter Monday (Pondělí velikonoční)

Easter Monday is different in the Czech Republic. Prague celebrates spring as men of all ages chase their favourite girls and swat them on the legs with ribboned willow switches; the girls respond with gifts of hand-painted eggs, then the party begins. Days of spring-cleaning and cooking precede this ritual.

APRIL

Burning of the Witches (Pálení čarodějnic)

There are various explanations of this pagan ritual, in which people burn brooms and light fires, but the most common is that it's designed to ward off evil. On 30 April there are burning brooms at Výstaviště (p133), plus bonfire parties on Kampa Island (p57) and, unofficially, up Petřín Hill (p59).

MAY

Labour Day (Svátek práce)

Sacred under the communists, 1 May is now mainly a chance for a holiday.

Prague Spring (Pražské jaro)

www.festival.cz

Prague's prestigious classical music festival begins 12 May, the anniversary of composer Bedřich Smetana's death. A procession goes from Vyšehrad to Smetana Hall in Municipal House, where Smetana's *Má Vlast* (My Country) opens the programme.

Prague International Marathon

www.pim.cz

Central Prague's streets are closed as 14,000 runners cover 42km (pictured below).

Prague Fringe

www.praguefringe.com, www.myspace
.com/praguefringe

English comedy, theatre and music nights take over Malá Strana in late May.

Khamoro

www.khamoro.cz

In late May Prague celebrates Roma culture, with traditional music, dance, art and a Staré Město parade.

JUNE

Dance Prague

www.tanecpha.cz

This international festival of modern dance is held across various theatres.

Prague Writers' Festival

www.pwf.cz

Although never quite living up to its billing as the literary 'Left Bank of the 1990s', Prague does attract huge names to this major European festival. Past attendees include Margaret Atwood, Jeffrey Eugenides, Yann Martel, Ian McEwan, Salman Rushdie and Susan Sontag.

JULY

Jan Hus Day (Den Jana Husa)

Celebrations on 6 July mark the burning at the stake of the great Bohemian religious reformer Jan Hus in 1415. There's also bell-ringing at Bethlehem Chapel (p71) the evening before.

Ameropa

www.ameropa.org

The sweet strains of chamber music can be heard across Prague from the last weekend of the month.

AUGUST

Festival of Italian Opera

www.opera.cz

Beginning in August and extending into September, this festival features the works of Verdi and other Italian composers. Performed at the Prague State Opera (p117), it provides a chance to see quality productions outside the main opera season.

SEPTEMBER

Prague Autumn (Pražský podzim)

www.prazskypodzim.cz

Orchestras from Germany and British broadcaster the BBC regularly attend this autumnal version of the Prague Spring classical music festival. The main venue is the Rudolfinum (p95).

FILM FESTIVALS

While the biggest Czech film festival is in Karolvy Vary in July (www.kviff.cz), Prague hosts these:

Days of European Film (www.euro filmfest.cz; Kino Světozor, p115, & other cinemas; Jan-Feb) This smorgasbord of new European film usually includes one all-night session.

Febiofest (www.febiofest.cz; cinemas across town; usually Mar) Showcasing international film, TV and video works from new and experienced directors.

One World (Jeden Svět; www.one world.cz; cinemas across town; usually Apr) A week of human-rights documentaries.

Burčak Wine Festivals

Burčak is the first sweet young wine to appear during autumn's grape harvesting and is only briefly available. Some of the biggest celebrations are in Vinohrady.

OCTOBER

International Jazz Festival (Mezinárodní Jazzový Festival)

www.jazzfestivalpraha.cz/_jazz

Established in 1964, but in its current form for just over 30 years, this two-week festival presents Czech musicians and star performers from around the world. Herbie Hancock and Acker Bilk have performed here. Inaugurated at the Reduta Jazz Club (p116), the festival has expanded into the Lucerna Music Bar (p115).

NOVEMBER

All Souls' Day

As Czechs light candles for the souls of the dead on 2 November, Prague's cemeteries – including Vyšehrad (p22) and Olšany (p121) – are particularly atmospheric.

Anniversary of the Velvet Revolution

While many young Czechs think 1989's revolution is ancient history, politicians and older Czechs still gather before memorials on 17 November (see p144).

DECEMBER

Christmas–New Year (Vánoce-Nový Rok)

December in Prague is magical, with a huge Christmas tree erected in the Old Town Sq beside a Christmas market (pictured below). More Christmas markets across town sell seasonal decorations, gifts and traditional foods, while stalls ladle out *svařák* mulled wine. Elsewhere, tanks of fat 'Christmas' carp await eager Czech customers.

>ITINERARIES

Ceiling of the Strahov Library (p46)

ITINERARIES

ONE DAY

Such an unusually short time scale demands an unorthodox approach. Alight at Můstek metro station (Václavské náměstí exit) and glance up Wenceslas Sq (p103) before turning down Na můstku. Turn right at Rytířská and left at the Estates Theatre (p93). Follow Železná to the Astronomical Clock (p71) and Old Town Sq. Note the Church of Our Lady Before Týn (p74) and then leave the square through its upper left (northwest) corner, passing Franz Kafka's birthplace (p75). Wander quickly through the Old Jewish Cemetery (p78). Head across uncrowded Mánesův Bridge, admiring neighbouring Charles Bridge (p56). Pop into the Wallenstein Garden (p62) and then head to the castle. Climb the tower of St Vitus Cathedral (p49). Phew. Time for a beer at U Černého Vola (p53), before settling on the terrace of Cowboys (p65) for lunch.

Continue downhill along Nerudova to Malostranské náměstí. Do a circular detour through southern Malá Strana. Head through Maltese Sq (p58), past the Lennon Wall (p58) and round Kampa Island. Maybe pop into the Kampa Museum (p57). If you're keen to actually cross Charles Bridge retrace your footsteps north, cross the river, follow the signs back to the Old Town Sq. Then continue to Municipal House (p75) for a late afternoon tea.

Alternatively, cross Legion Bridge at the south of Kampa Island and take a seat in Kavárna Slavia (p112) or Café Louvre (p108). Choose a pub for the evening – perhaps Baráčnická rychta or upstairs at U Medvídků (p91). Having ticked off eight Prague highlights or more before 6pm, give yourself an award for speed-tourism.

TWO DAYS

If you know you've got two days, you can take a slower pace. This time start at Prague Castle (p10) and spend a few hours here, before wandering downhill along Nerudova. Head under Charles Bridge (right off Mostecká at Lázeňská, left into Saska and onwards in U lužického). Laugh at the 'Piss' sculpture (p62) at Cihelná, before treating yourself to a slap-up lunch at Hergetova Cihelná (p66). Head north to see the Wallenstein Garden (p18) and then cross the river via Mánesův Bridge. Stop in the

---

Top left John Lennon bust, Lennon Wall (p58) **Top right** Kafka in Prague **Bottom** Crowds gather in the Old Town Sq to watch the Astronomical Clock chime on the hour (p71)

FORWARD PLANNING

Accommodation and flights in summer aside, Prague isn't a city that requires the visitor to do much planning. Indeed, it almost discourages it. Many major sights aren't ticketed, and even a major attraction like Municipal House simply won't take bookings for building tours before the actual day.

If you're coming to attend a major festival such as Prague Spring (p27), check the website at least a month beforehand. If you want to see some opera, classical or rock music, two weeks or so before you come to Prague, log onto sites like www.praguepost.com, www .prague.tv, www.expats.cz and www.ticketpro.cz just to see what's on. The bulk of opera and classical music tickets are sold the day before a performance. (Although this might be different for a star appearance, we've previously obtained tickets to a highly rated philharmonic performance just hours before curtain call.)

We've noted in individual reviews where you might want to book restaurants. If you're coming for Valentine's Day, booking a week or two ahead is a good idea. Otherwise, a phone call the night before, or even the morning of the same day, should be the most required.

Old Jewish Cemetery (p13), then head through the Old Town Sq to cubist Grand Café Orient (p90). The evening is yours, for dining, pubbing, clubbing or culture – check the Snapshots chapter (p146) for ideas.

If you can get up early the next morning, cross Charles Bridge and head south into Kampa Island (p57). If not, catch a tram (6, 9, 12, 20, 22, or 23) to Újezd. Mosey around the streets here, and possibly visit the

Stop for afternoon tea in the cubist Grand Café Orient (p90)

Kampa Museum (p57). Then take the funicular up Petřín Hill and walk to Strahov Monastery (p19).

In the afternoon, head to Wenceslas Sq (p16). Look at the nearby sights – the Jan Palach Memorial (p100), the Wenceslas Statue (p105), Lucerna Passage (p100) and the cubist lamppost (p97) – before heading back towards the Old Town for a spot of souvenir shopping (p158).

Have dinner in Hot (p109), to get you into the clubbing mood. Move on briefly to somewhere like Bombay (p89) or Chateau (p93), before heading to Roxy (p94), M1 (p93), Radost FX (p128) or Mecca (p138), depending on your tastes and mood.

FOUR DAYS

Follow the Two Days itinerary, then rise late on day three and collect some supplies in Bakeshop Praha (p84) or Tesco (p107) before recovering with a leisurely picnic atop Vyšehrad (p22). Refreshed, do something soothing this evening like attending a classical concert (see p156).

Day four starts with an exploration of Vinohrady and Žižkov. Admire the Church of the Most Sacred Heart of Our Lord (p120) and wander to the base of the nearby Žižkov Tower (p121) to look at the giant babies crawling up it. If you're a Kafka fan, get back on the metro and visit his grave in the Jewish Cemetery (p120).

After lunch – try Ambiente (p123) – catch a tram to Veletržní Palace (p133; the quickest route is a green-line metro to Malostranská, then tram 12). Afterwards wander back to Letná Gardens (p132). End your visit to Prague in the beer garden here, supping a Gambrinus while watching the sun set on this magnificent city.

RAINY DAY

Prague isn't great when it's wet; those cobblestones become quite slippery. But for those who aren't thrilled by an entire day of drinking (also an option), scenic tram 22 rides to the rescue. Pick up the tram outside Národní třída metro or at nearby Kavárna Slavia (p112). Stick with it – across the river, past Petřín, Malá Strana and the castle – at least until it reaches the Pražský hrad stop, before returning. Or take the one-hour round-trip to Bílá Hora and back. Alight again at Národní třída, change to the metro to Náměstí Republiky, and take refuge in Municipal House (p21).

After a coffee, meal or tour of the building, scurry to nearby Slovanksy dům mall (p107), where there are shops, restaurants and cinemas. Hop from

Malostranská metro station

ITINERARIES

Relax at the Letná Beer Garden (p135)

mall to covered mall along this street until you reach Wenceslas Sq. Head undercover again in Lucerna Passage (p100) and Kavárna Lucerna (p112).

From here, it's just another quick dash to Novoměstský Pivovar (p112) for some food and good Czech beer.

For an alternative rainy-day itinerary, see p24.

FOR FREE

On a clear day, some of the best things in Prague cost nothing – at least once you've bought a public transport ticket (see p178). At Prague Castle (p46) the views from the gardens are priceless, and St Vitus Cathedral is no longer pay-per-view either (see the boxed text, p47). The Nový Svět Quarter (p46) is a cost-free alternative to the castle's Golden Lane, and the walk between Petřín Hill and Strahov Monastery (p19) is one of the nicest things in town to do. Indeed most of the city's highlights don't cost a bean. You can generally admire Prague's architecture and even spy the Old Jewish Cemetery for free (see the boxed text, p79).

You're not missing much if you don't visit many museums. Some of the best, the Kampa Museum (p57), the Museum of Decorative Arts (p76) and Veletržní Palace (p133) have free entry at certain times; see reviews for details. In the Mucha Museum (p101) you can also admire the artist's work simply by browsing through the shop.

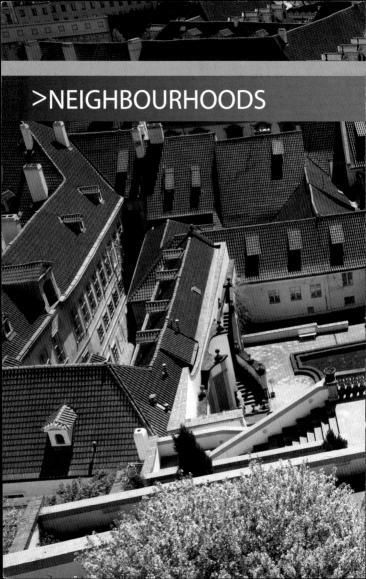

>NEIGHBOURHOODS

The gardens below Prague Castle (p50)

NEIGHBOURHOODS

Franz Kafka – ever the eternal optimist – used to complain that everything in Prague was small and cramped.

For short-term visitors, however, the city's petite dimensions are a distinct blessing, enabling them to get from A to Z and back in just about an afternoon. (Although given Prague's multilayered nature, you'll probably want to retrace your steps repeatedly, uncovering more each time before you leave.)

Fittingly perhaps, given the Kafka connection, the Vltava River makes a giant question mark through the middle of Prague, with the city centre nestled near the underside of the curlicue. Nine bridges straddle this waterway, linking areas like Hradčany (the medieval castle district) and Malá Strana (the 'Little Quarter') on the left bank with Staré Město (the Old Town), Nové Město (the New Town) and the ancient citadel of Vyšehrad on the right.

Prague's first two settlements were formed at the polar extremes of this area, with the 9th-century castle at Hradčany and a 10th-century citadel at Vyšehrad. Gradually, over hundreds of years, the central city districts sidled together.

Cute, winding Malá Strana formed at the foot of the hill as early as the 10th century as a satellite suburb to Hradčany. Meanwhile, independent merchants had established the equally labyrinthine Staré Město across the river. This 'Old Town' contained the walled Jewish ghetto and the unwalled Jewish district of Josefov that replaced it in the 19th century.

Boulevard-lined Nové Město was bolted onto Staré Město in the 14th century, completing the central jigsaw. Yet Prague needed more room to grow even after this. The royal vineyards at Vinohrady were finally built upon in the late 19th century; working-class and industrial districts like Holešovice in the north, Smíchov in the west and Žižkov in the east were established at this time, too. In 21st-century Prague, interestingly, it's those last three quarters that are consistently described as up-and-coming as money is slowly being spent on and in them.

HRADČANY (p43)

Dejvice

Malá Strana

MALÁ STRANA (p55)

Smíchov

Letná

Vltava River

Josefov

Staré Město

STARÉ MĚSTO (pp72-3)

HOLEŠOVICE (p131)

Holešovice

Karlín

Nové Město

NOVÉ MĚSTO & VYŠEHRAD (pp98-9)

Vyšehrad

Žižkov

VINOHRADY & ŽIŽKOV (p119)

Vinohrady

1 km
0.5 miles

0
0

> HRADČANY

If Prague Castle dominates Prague, then it certainly overshadows this district – and usually literally. From Strahov Monastery to the baroque convent of the Loreta, the spires of St Vitus Cathedral at the castle's heart are rarely out of view. Even in the hollow of the Nový Svět Quarter, where sightlines are obscured, you're still conscious of the royal omnipresence; after all, this doll-sized enclave was built for the castle's hard-working medieval minions.

Hradčany (the castle district) might be slightly older than previously believed. Recent archaeological finds suggest the castle could have been built at the very start of the 9th century, rather than the previously cited 870. But no matter, for what's not in any dispute is the castle's size (more than seven football fields) and majesty. And the neighbours have simply had to keep up.

Devastated in the Great Fire of 1541, Hradčany was rebuilt in Renaissance style, and Habsburg empire nobles used the opportunity to ring the castle with impressive palaces. You'll still see these around Hradčany Sq (Hradčanské náměstí) at the castle's main gate.

HRADČANY

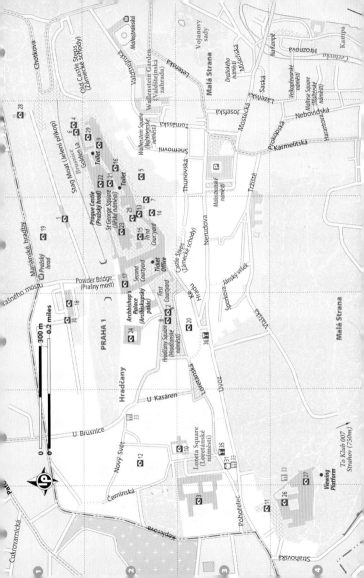

SEE
ČERNIN PALACE

Černinský palác; Loretánské náměstí; 🚊 **22, 23 to Pohořelec**

Prague is infamous for defenestrations (see the boxed text, opposite), where hapless political opponents have been hurtled from windows. One occurred here. In 1948 Jan Masaryk – son of first Czechoslovak president Tomáš Masaryk and the only non-communist in the post-war government – 'fell' to his death from his top-floor bathroom. Used as SS headquarters during WWII, the 17th-century building now houses the foreign ministry.

HRADČANY SQUARE

Hradčanské náměstí; Ⓜ **Malostranská or** 🚊 **22, 23 to Pohořelec or Brusnice**

Hradčany Sq, before Prague Castle's main gates (see p46), is dominated by the striking black-and-white *sgraffito* façade of the 18th-century **Schwarzenberg Palace** (Schwarzenberský palác). From late 2007 this will house part of the National Gallery, although it's going to be hard to upstage the 3D optical illusion of its own exterior. For fans of 14th- to 18th-century European art, the nearby **Sternberg Palace** (☎ 222 321 459; www .ngprague.cz; adult/concession150/70Kč; ☾ 10am-6pm Tue-Sun) already hosts National Gallery works by

Admire the ceiling fresco of the Strahov Library (p46)

FALLING OUT OF WINDOWS

Czechs weren't the first to practise 'defenestration' but they've certainly had an unfortunate history of people involuntarily plummeting from windows.

The so-called First Defenestration of Prague was due to religious in-fighting. It occurred in 1419 when Protestants, still angry about the execution of their leader Jan Hus four years earlier (see p166), threw several Catholic councillors from Prague's New Town Hall.

The Second Defenestration of Prague in 1618 proved even more devastating. Again, Protestant nobles rebelling against the Catholic Habsburg emperor tossed two councillors and a secretary out of a Prague Castle window (see p48). However, this sectarian act sparked off the Europe-wide Thirty Years' War. It might be pure legend that the defenestrated councillors and secretary lived by falling into the dung-filled moat, but the entire continent most definitely landed in the proverbial.

Besides Jan Masaryk's 1948 defenestration from Černin Palace (see opposite), other instances include that of novelist Bohumil Hrabal (see p172). In a surreal twist befitting one of his own stories, Hrabal died in 1997 when he fell from a 5th-floor hospital window while feeding pigeons.

Breughel, Dürer, Goya, Rembrandt and Rubens.

◉ LORETA

☎ 224 516 740; www.loreta.cz; Loretánské náměstí 7; adult/concession 110/90Kč; ☷ 9am-12.15pm & 1-4.30pm Tue-Sun, weekly church services 7.30pm Sat & 6pm Sun; 🚊 22, 23 to Pohořelec

A crucified, bearded lady and the skeletons of two Spanish saints are found in this baroque place of pilgrimage. At its heart is a 15th-century replica **Santa Casa** (Sacred House); the original was supposedly the home of the Virgin Mary, carried by angels to the Italian town of Loreto, and this model allegedly contains a few elements from the original. Elsewhere, the Loreta's eye-popping treasury contains the 90cm-tall **Prague Sun** (Pražské slunce) studded with 6222 diamonds.

◉ MINIATURES MUSEUM

Muzeum miniatur; ☎ 233 352 371; Strahov Monastery; adult/child 50/30Kč; ☷ 10am-5pm; 🚊 22, 23 to Pohořelec

This collection of miniature artworks remains one of Prague's quirky gems. Peer through microscopes to see a flea with golden horseshoes and tiny camels biblically passing through the eye of a needle. Alternatively, raise a magnifying glass to miniature reproduction paintings and the world's smallest book, painstakingly created by Siberian optical technician Anatoly Konyenko over many years.

⊙ NOVÝ SVĚT QUARTER

Nový Svět, Černínská & around; 🚋 **22, 23 to Brusnice**

In the 16th century, houses were built for castle staff in an enclave of curving cobblestone streets down the slope north of the Loreta. Today these diminutive cottages have been restored and painted in pastel shades, making the 'New World' Quarter a perfect alternative to the castle's crowded Golden Lane. Danish astronomer Tycho Brahe (see p75) lived at No 1 Kapucínská. Internationally renowned animator and filmmaker Jan Švankmajer (see p173) resides at No 5 Černínská.

⊙ STRAHOV MONASTERY

Strahovská klášter; ☎ **233 107 718; www.strahovmonastery.cz; Strahovské nádvoří 1; adult/concession 80/50Kč;** 🕐 **9am-noon & 1-5pm;** 🚋 **22, 23 to Pohořelec**

Apart from magnificent views over Prague (see p19), Strahov Monastery's main drawcard is the baroque **Strahov Library** (Strahovská knihovna). This is divided into two magnificent book-lined halls – the two-storey high **Philosophy Hall** (Filozofický sál; 1780–97), with its grandiose ceiling fresco, and the stucco-encrusted **Theology Hall** (Teologický sál; 1679). For conservation reasons you can only peek through the doors but the connecting hall also contains a

Cabinet of Curiosities full of shrivelled sea creatures.

⊙ PRAGUE CASTLE

Known simply as *hrad* to proud Czechs, **Prague Castle** (Pražský hrad; ☎ 224 373 368, 224 372 434; www.hrad .cz; 🕐 buildings 9am-5pm Apr-Oct, to 4pm Nov-Mar, grounds 5am-midnight Apr-Oct, 9am-11pm Nov-Mar) was founded by 9th-century Přemysl princes and grew haphazardly as subsequent rulers made additions. Today it's a huge complex, proceeding west to east through a series of three courtyards. There have been four major reconstructions, most importantly by Slovene architect Jože Plečník after WWI. Hired by the first Czechoslovak president, Tomáš Masaryk, Plečník made the castle more user-friendly and created some memorable features. All Czech rulers have had their residence here, except the first post-communist president, Václav Havel: in 1989 he plumped for the comforts of his own home instead. See the boxed text, opposite, for transport and pricing details, and p10 for more on the castle.

⊙ CASTLE ENTRANCE

First Courtyard; admission free; 🕐 **5am-midnight Apr-Oct, 9am-11pm Nov-Mar;** Ⓜ **Malostranská or** 🚋 **22, 23 to Pohořelec or Brusnice**

VISITING PRAGUE CASTLE

There are several transport routes to the castle, but the choices fall into two main camps. On the one hand, you can catch a metro to Malostranská or tram 12, 20, 22 or 23 to Malostranská náměstí and face a stiff uphill walk to the impressive main gate. Alternatively, for an easy, level walk, you can take tram 22 or 23 to the Pražský hrad stop and the Powder Bridge. Hradčanská metro station is 10 minutes away, but also on an even keel.

Tickets to Prague Castle are valid for two days, although you may visit each attraction only once. The main information office is in the Third Courtyard, but there are others and they're all hard to miss.

Entrance to St Vitus Cathedral is once again free, after a legal battle saw it returned to the Czech State from the fee-charging Catholic Church in 2007. However, more wrangling is possible, so conceivably this could change once more.

Other attractions not covered below also levy separate entry fees, listed in individual reviews. Entry is free to the castle courtyards and gardens. Bank on spending at least two hours. Audioguides (145/180Kč for two/three hours) and guided tours (100Kč) are also available.

Prague Castle – long tour (adult/concession/family 350/175/500Kč) Includes Old Royal Palace, Story of Prague Castle, St George's Basilica, St George's Convent, Golden Lane with Daliborka Tower

Prague Castle – short tour (adult/concession/family 250/125/300Kč) Includes Old Royal Palace, St George's Basilica, Golden Lane with Daliborka Tower

The castle's main gate, on Hradčany Sq, is flanked by huge, 18th-century statues of **battling Titans**, which dwarf the guards beneath. Playwright-turned-president Václav Havel brought some pizzazz to the castle after 1989, when he hired the Czech costume designer on the film *Amadeus* to redesign the guards' uniforms and then instigated a **changing of the guard** ceremony. This takes place every hour between 5am and 10pm (9am and 10pm in winter), but the most impressive display is at noon, when banners are exchanged and a band plays.

🅖 GOLDEN LANE

Zlatá ulička; long or short tour tickets; 🕙 9am-5pm Apr-Oct, to 4pm Nov-Mar

The tiny, colourful cottages along this cobbled alley were built in the 16th century for the castle guard's sharpshooters, but were later used by goldsmiths, squatters and artists, including writer Franz Kafka (who stayed at his sister's house at No 22 from 1916 to 1917). Today the lane is lined with souvenir shops, but is still faintly charming if you arrive early or in low season. Skip the laughable torture exhibition in the **Daliborka Tower** at the eastern end.

⊙ LOBKOWICZ PALACE

Lobkovický palác; ☎ 257 535 979; Jiřská 3; admission free; ⏱ 10.30am-6pm

This 16th-century aristocratic residence reopened in 2007 with a collection of Renaissance paintings, musical instruments and some manuscripts by Mozart and Beethoven. Among the paintings are one of Velázquez's 'Infantas', Pieter Brueghel the Elder's 'Haymaking', and two panoramas of London, painted by Canaletto before 1666's Great Fire.

⊙ OLD ROYAL PALACE

Starý královský palác; Third Courtyard; long & short tour tickets; ⏱ 9am-5pm Apr-Oct, 9am-4pm Nov-Mar; Ⓜ Malostranská

The highlight here is the high-Gothic vaulted roof of **Vladislav Hall** (Vladislavský sál; 1493–1502), beneath which all the presidents of the republic have been sworn in. There's also a balcony off the hall with great city views and a door to the former **Bohemian Chancellery** (České kanceláře), where the

Fairy-tale Prague Castle (p46) dominates the city skyline

so-called Second Defenestration of Prague occurred (see p45).

☉ PLEČNÍK MONOLITH
Third Courtyard
A noteworthy feature near St Vitus Cathedral is a huge granite monolith dedicated to the victims of WWI, designed by Slovene architect Jože Plečník in 1928. Nearby is a copy of the castle's famous **statue of St George** slaying the dragon; the original 14th-century bronze statue is now in the Story of Prague Castle exhibition.

☉ PRAGUE CASTLE PICTURE GALLERY
Obrazárna pražského hradu; ☎ 224 373 531; Second Courtyard; adult/concession 150/80Kč; ⏲ 9am-5pm Apr-Oct, to 4pm Nov-Mar
In 1648 an invading Swedish army looted Emperor Rudolf II's art collection (as well as making off with the original bronze statues in the Wallenstein Garden, p18). These converted Renaissance stables house what was left plus replacement works, including some by Rubens, Tintoretto and Titian.

☉ ROYAL GARDEN
Královská zahrada; North of Second Courtyard
The **Powder Bridge** (Prašný most; 1540) spans the **Stag Moat** (Jelení příkop) en route to the spacious, Renaissance-style Royal Garden. This started life in 1534 and its most beautiful building is the **Ball-Game House** (Míčovna; 1569), a masterpiece of Renaissance *sgraffito* where the Habsburgs once played an early form of badminton. To the east is the **Summer Palace** (Letohrádek; 1538–60) and to the west the former **Riding School** (jízdárna; 1695).

☉ ST GEORGE'S BASILICA
Bazilika sv Jiří; Jiřské náměstí; long & short tour tickets; ⏲ 9am-5pm Apr-Oct, to 4pm Nov-Mar
Behind a brick-red façade lies the Czech Republic's best-preserved Romanesque church. The original was established in the 10th century by Vratislav I (the father of St Wenceslas), who is still buried here, as is St Ludmilla. All in all, it's quite a sparse venue, popular for small concert performances.

☉ ST GEORGE'S CONVENT
Klášter sv Jiří; ☎ 257 320 536; Jiřské náměstí 33; adult/concession/family 100/50/150Kč; ⏲ 10am-6pm Tue-Sun
Bohemia's first convent, established in 973, now contains yet another branch of the National Gallery. There's an extensive collection of Renaissance and baroque art here.

☉ ST VITUS CATHEDRAL
Chrám sv Víta; Third Courtyard; ⏲ 9am-5pm Apr-Oct, to 4pm Nov-Mar

Although it was begun in 1344 and appears Gothic to the very tips of its pointy spires, much of St Vitus Cathedral was only completed in time for its belated consecration in 1929. Once you've passed through the **Golden Gate** main doorway, with its 14th-century **mosaic of the Last Judgment**, you'll receive a small brochure of highlights. Of these, the bird's-eye view from the 96m-tall **Great Tower** more than repays the strenuous effort of climbing the 297 steps. And don't miss the **Art Nouveau**

stained-glass window by Alfons Mucha (see p100), the baroque, silver **tomb of St John of Nepomuk** with its draped canopy and cherubs, or the ornate **Chapel of St Wenceslas**.

☉ SOUTHERN GARDENS

Jižní zahrady; ⏱ 10am-6pm Apr-Oct, closed winter; Ⓜ Malostranská

The three gardens lined up below the castle's southern wall – **Paradise Garden**, the **Hartig Garden** and the **Garden on the Ramparts** – offer superb views over Malá Strana's rooftops and even a glimpse into the British embassy's back garden. The two main gardens, Paradise Garden and the Garden on the Ramparts, were landscaped in the 1920s by Slovene architect Jože Plečnik, and Paradise Garden has an obelisk marking where the victims of the second defenestration of Prague fell (see p45). You can approach this contiguous bit of greenery from the west via the New Castle Steps into Paradise Garden or from the east via the Old Castle Steps into the Garden on the Ramparts. A third route, the Bull Steps, takes you from the Third Courtyard into the Garden on the Ramparts.

☉ STORY OF PRAGUE CASTLE

☎ 224 373 102; www.story-castle .cz; long-tour ticket or adult/concession 140/70Kč; ⏱ 9am-6pm Apr-Oct, to 4pm Nov-Mar

---

CURSE OF THE CZECH CROWN JEWELS

In St Vitus Cathedral, on the southern side of the Chapel of St Wenceslas, there's a small door locked with seven keys. In a nod to the seven seals of Revelations, each is in the safekeeping of a separate official.

What lies beyond this secretive and carefully guarded door? The Czech crown jewels, of course. They're rarely exhibited to the public, but the oldest among them is the 22-carat gold St Wenceslas Crown, made for Charles IV in 1347 and dedicated to the earlier prince.

Like all the best regal artefacts, the crown comes with a legendary curse; any usurper wearing it is doomed to die within the year. Call it coincidence, but the Nazi chief in Prague, Reinhard Heydrich, donned the crown in 1941 and was duly assassinated in 1942 by the resistance (see p102).

This is one of the castle's newest and most compelling exhibitions, with displays expertly presented in a low-lit, state-of-the-art environment and explained in English. The collection of armour, jewellery, glassware, furniture and other artefacts traces more than 1000 years of castle history. One outstanding sight is the skeleton of the pre-Christian 'warrior', still encased in the earth where archaeologists found him within the castle grounds.

◻ TOY MUSEUM
Muzeum hražek; ☎ 224 372 294; Jiřská 6; adult/concession 50/30Kč; ☒ 9.30am-5.30pm

Frivolous but fun, this exhibition runs the gamut from model trains, robots, teddy bears and wooden dolls to colourful German tambourines and tiny tin horses with whistles in their tails. Most strikingly, the upper floor has been invaded and colonised by hundreds of Barbie dolls (including celebrity lookalikes). If taking children, be aware the entire collection is hands-off.

◻ TUNNEL
Apr-Oct only; ☒ 22, 23 to Pražský hrad

In 2002 an arty new tunnel – red-brick and rather Freudian – was completed by architect Josef Pleskot beneath the castle's Powder Bridge, making a quirky

alternative exit route from the castle. Turn west (left) from the bridge's castle side and follow the footpath down into the moat to reach it. If you keep going, you'll reach Malostranská metro.

SHOP
◻ ROCKING HORSE TOY SHOP
Toys

hračky – houpací kůň; ☎ 603 515 745; cztoy@yahoo.com; Loretánské náměstí 3; ☒ 9.30am-6.30pm; ☒ 22, 23 to Pohořelec

A cut above, this wonderful shop is palpably a labour of love for discerning owner Ivan Karhan, who's assembled high-quality wooden carved folk dolls (from leading regions like Krouňa, Přibram and Skašov), old 1950s wind-up steel tractors, toy cars and even a few rocking horses. For a typically Czech souvenir, the famous and ubiquitous Little Mole character is here in several guises, but this small store also stocks quality toys and art supplies you won't find elsewhere in the city.

🍴 EAT
Many of the restaurants near the castle are overpriced tourist traps, and you'll have a far greater choice if you head down the hill to Malá Strana (p64).

Bring out your inner child at the Rocking Horse Toy Shop (p51)

🍴 BELLAVISTA *Italian* $$$
☎ 220 517 274; www.kolkovna.cz; Strahovské nádvoří 1; 11am-midnight Mar-Oct, closed Nov-Feb; 🚋 22, 23 to Pohořelec

There are several restaurants in and around the Strahov Monastery, all aimed squarely at overseas visitors. This, however, does boast a terrace with amazing views, and is upmarket enough to have served the Rolling Stones and Sean Connery. Hell, even the Italian food gets good reviews.

🍴 MALÝ BUDDHA *Asian* $
☎ 220 513 894; Úvoz 46; 🕑 noon-10.30pm Tue-Sun; 🚋 22, 23 to Pohořelec; Ⓥ

Candlelight, incense and a Buddhist shrine characterise this cosy, vaulted restaurant, which hints at an Eastern tearoom. The menu boasts Thai, Chinese and – unusually for Prague – Vietnamese dishes, many of them vegetarian. Drinks include ginseng wine, coconut and mango juices and nearly 40 kinds of tea.

🍴 U ZLATÉ HRUŠKY *Czech* $$$$
☎ 220 514 778; Nový Svět 3; 🕑 11.30am-3pm & 6.30pm-midnight; 🚋 22, 23 to Brusnice

Treat yourself to beautifully prepared Czech and international dishes at this fastidious restaurant in the romantic Nový Svět Quarter. 'At the Golden Pear' is frequented as much by locals and visiting dignitaries as it is by tourists. In summer you can opt for a table in its leafy *zahradní restaurace* (garden restaurant) across the street.

DRINK

U ČERNÉHO VOLA *Pub*
☎ 220 513 481; Loretánské náměstí 1; ☾ 10am-10pm; ☒ 22, 23 to Pohořelec
Being the sort of bar where locals stare at new faces (ie yours), the wonderful 'Black Ox' has managed to maintain an authentic atmosphere right on a tourist strip. The long tables, coats of arms and drinkers staring into their delicious Kozel beer make it feel ancient; in fact, it was built after WWII. The major pity is it closes so early.

U ZAVĚŠENÝHO KAFE *Bar*
☎ 605 294 595; www.uzavesenyhokafe.com; Úvoz 6; ☾ 11am-midnight; ☒ 22, 23 to Pohořelec

The 'Hanging Coffee Cup' is named after the charming old practice of buying an extra mug on the off chance a poor fellow customer might need it, and there's certainly a collegiate feel in this legendary superb drinking den. The cosy wood-panelled back room, with its weird art and '60s jukebox, is the best spot to enjoy the beer, coffee and pub grub offered.

PLAY

KLUB 007 STRAHOV *Club*
☎ 257 211 439; www.myspace.com/klub 007strahov; Block 7, Chaloupeckého 7; cover 50-250Kč; ☾ 7pm-1am Sun-Thu, to 2am Fri & Sat; ☒ 143, 176, 217
Klub 007 is a grungy student club in the basements of one of the big dormitory blocks in Strahov, near the rundown Strahov Stadium. The legendary 007 has been around since 1987, when it was a focus for underground music, and is now famed for its devotion to hardcore, punk and ska.

> MALÁ STRANA

Slipping down the hillside from the castle to Charles Bridge, Malá Strana ('Lesser Town' or 'Little Quarter') is one of Prague's most trafficked districts. The main thoroughfare is the steep street of Nerudova. However, beyond this lies a picturesque network of winding cobblestone streets and quaint, colourful buildings (see also p11).

Malá Strana has had many incarnations. A market town, it became the medieval home of German craftsmen, and after the Great Fire of 1541 it was destroyed and rebuilt. Its Renaissance architecture was given a baroque makeover in the 17th and 18th centuries, whence it derives its current look – from the green-domed Church of St Nicholas to the impressive Wallenstein Garden and other features.

By then a bohemian quarter befitting of its 'left bank' position, it was a temporary home to Mozart and Casanova. Many of its noble palaces are now embassies, and sit alongside reminders of other early residents, like the Knights of Malta.

MALÁ STRANA

👁 SEE
Charles Bridge................ **1** F2
Church of Our Lady
Victorious...................... **2** E3
Church of St Nicholas **3** D2
Franz Kafka Museum **4** F2
Kampa Island **5** F3
Kampa Museum **6** F3
Lennon Wall **7** E2
Maltese Square **8** E3
Memorial to the Victims
of Communism **9** D4
Nerudova...................... **10** D2
Petřín (Štefanik)
Observatory **11** C4
Petřín Funicular............ **12** D4
Petřín Lookout Tower... **13** B3
Petřín Mirror Maze...... **14** C3
'Piss' Sculpture............. **15** F2

'Quo Vadis' Sculpture... **16** C2
Wallenstein Garden **17** E1

🏠 SHOP
Manufaktura **18** E2
Manufaktura **19** D2
Material....................... **20** F2
Pavla & Olga................ **21** C2

🍴 EAT
Bar Bar........................ **22** E4
Bohemia Bagel............. **23** E4
Café Savoy **24** E4
Cowboys...................... **25** C2
Cukrkávalimonáda **26** E2
Gitanes....................... **27** D2
Hergetova Cihelná **28** F2
Kampa Park **29** F2
Pálffy Palác **30** E1

Restaurant Nebozízek.. **31** C4
Square **32** E2
U Maltézských Rytířů... **33** E2
U Modré Kachničky **34** E3
U Zlaté Studné............. **35** E1

🍷 DRINK
Baráčnická Rychta........ **36** D2
Blue Light.................... **37** E2
Mill Kavárna **38** E4
St Nicholas Café........... **39** D2
U Kocoura **40** D2

⭐ PLAY
Klub Újezd **41** E4
PopoCaféPetl Music
Club **42** E4
U Malého Glena........... **43** E2

SEE

CHARLES BRIDGE

Karlův most; admission free; 🕙 24hr;
🚃 12, 20, 22, 23 to Malostranské náměstí
Big plans are afoot for the most
popular thoroughfare across
the Vltava River, connecting
Malá Strana and Staré Město. A
100-million Kč renovation of the
650-year-old stone bridge began in
2007 and might run into 2008. During work, either the left or right side
will be roped off at any one time,
creating an even tighter bottleneck.
For more on the bridge see p12.

CHURCH OF OUR LADY VICTORIOUS

Kostel Panny Marie Vítězné; 🕿 257 533
646; www.pragjesu.info; Karmelitská 9;
admission by donation; 🕙 8.30am-7pm
Mon-Sat, to 8pm Sun, closed 25 Dec &
Easter Mon; 🚃 12, 20, 22, 23 to Hellichova
When a miracle-working 'Bambino
di Praga' statue appears in classic
Czech novel *I served the King of
England,* it sounds purely fictional.
Yet this church really does contain
a 400-year-old, wax 'Baby Jesus
of Prague', said to have protected
the city for centuries. The tradition
of dressing the 47cm-tall figure

Explore the novelist's relationship with Prague in the Franz Kafka Museum

from a wardrobe of 70 costumes continues today, with nuns changing his robes according to a religious calendar.

CHURCH OF ST NICHOLAS

Kostel sv Mikuláše; Malostranské náměstí 38; adult/child 60/30Kč; 9am-5pm Mar-Oct, 9am-4pm Nov-Feb; 12, 20, 22, 23 to Malostranské náměstí

Malá Strana is dominated by the huge green cupola of Prague's finest baroque building. Begun by famous Bavarian architect Kristof Dientzenhofer and continued by his son Kilian, the church boasts Europe's largest fresco, Johann Kracker's 1770 *Apotheosis of St Nicholas,* on its ceiling.

FRANZ KAFKA MUSEUM

Muzeum Franzy Kafky; 257 535 507; www.kafkamuseum.cz; Hergetova Cihelná 2b; adult/child 120/60Kč; 10am-6pm; M Malostranská

Don't be deterred by the Oedipus-complex psychobabble at the start of this modern museum. Go with the flow. Enjoy the trippy movie about Prague, the exhibits that curve through translucent netting, the rows of filing cabinets, a claustrophobic, strobe-lit section and original documents and photos. Although some call it pretentious and it's more fulfilling for speakers of Kafka's native German, no seri-

PRAGUE'S LITTLE VENICE

A lovely little green oasis, Kampa Island is separated from Malá Strana proper by a canal known as the Devil's Stream (Čertovka). Two mill wheels survive, where washerwomen used to do laundry until the 1930s. Nowadays, the island attracts young families, dog-walkers and artists. Night-time views of the lights twinkling across the river are superb, particularly from the south of the island. Take tram 6, 9, 12, 20, 22 or 23 to Újezd.

ous fan will want to miss this. For more on Kafka, see p17 & p142.

KAMPA MUSEUM

Muzeum Kampa; 257 286 147; www.museumkampa.cz; U sovových mlýnů 2; adult/child 120/60Kč, Mon free; 10am-6pm; 6, 9, 12, 20, 22, 23 to Újezd

Its prime location on the Vltava's left bank makes this flour-mill turned gallery as attractive as the work it contains. So while acquainting yourself with Otto Gutfreund's cubist sculptures, František Kupka paintings and other modern Central European art, don't forget to enjoy the roof terrace and eyrie facing Petřín Hill. The huge wooden chair on the wall in the river is best viewed through the small concave mirror in one of the galleries or from the riverside terrace café in summer.

○ LENNON WALL

Velkopřevorské náměstí; ⊞ 12, 20, 22, 23 to Malostranské náměstí

Dissidents in communist Czecho-slovakia often revered Western rock musicians like John Lennon for flouting social norms. And after Lennon's 1980 murder this wall was painted with his image and turned into a graffiti-splattered memorial – repainted each time the secret police whitewashed over it. Today the wall looks like any other graffiti-splattered monument. You might pass it several times before realising what it is.

○ MALTESE SQUARE

Maltézské náměstí; ⊞ 12, 20, 22, 23 to Malostranské náměstí

References to the Knights of Malta around Malá Strana hark back to 1169, when that military order established a monastery in the Church of Our Lady Beneath the Chain on this square. Disbanded by the communists, the Knights have regained much property under post-1989 restitution laws, including the Lennon Wall.

○ MEMORIAL TO THE VICTIMS OF COMMUNISM

Památník obětem komunismu; foot of Petřín Hill; ⊞ 6, 9, 12, 20, 22, 23 to Újezd

Get up close and personal with the sculptures at the Kampa Museum (p57)

THE NUMBERS GAME

Until numbering was introduced in the 18th century, exotic house names and signs were the only way of identifying individual Prague buildings. This practice came to a halt in 1770 when it was banned by the city fathers.

More such-named houses and signs survive in Nerudova than along any other Prague street. As you head downhill look out for: At the Two Suns (No 47), the Golden Horseshoe (No 34), the Three Fiddles (No12), the Red Eagle (No 6) and the Devil (No 4). Other signs include a St Wenceslas on horseback (number 34), a golden key (number 27) and a golden goblet (number 16).

This striking sculpture by Olbram Zoubek has male figures in various stages of desiccation descending a concrete staircase. Below them, a metal line down the centre of the steps counts the victims: 327 shot while trying to escape across the border, 170,938 driven into exile, 205,486 arrested, 248 executed and 4500 who died in prison.

◉ NERUDOVA

🚋 12, 20, 22, 23 to Malostranské náměstí
Malá Strana's main thoroughfare plunges steeply downhill from the castle to Malostranské náměstí. Today it's lined with touristy restaurants and shops, but you can still admire the 'baroque-ified' Renaissance façades and ornate old house signs (see the boxed text, left). Casanova and Mozart shared lodgings in 1791 at No 33, Bretfeldský Palace. Czech writer Jan Neruda, after whom the street takes its current name, lived at No 47, At the Two Suns (1845–57).

◉ PETŘÍN FUNICULAR

Lanová dráha; ⏱ 9am to 11.20pm;
🚋 6, 9, 12, 22, 20, 23 to Újezd
While you can walk up Petřín along several routes – from Hradčany via Strahov or directly from Újezd – by far the most fun way to arrive is on this funicular railway from Újezd. Services leave every 15 to 20 minutes. Ordinary public transport tickets are valid, but drivers always seem keen to help if you need it.

◉ PETŘÍN HILL

Petřín funicular
Most attractions atop this lookout point were built in the late 19th to early 20th century, creating a slightly innocent, fun-fair atmosphere. The huge stone fortifications that run from Újezd to Strahov, cutting across Petřín's peak, are different. This so-called Hunger Wall was built in 1362 under Charles IV, constructed by the city's poor in return for food under an early job-creation scheme.

NEIGHBOURHOODS

MALÁ STRANA

Climb the 299 steps up Petřín Lookout Tower for magnificent views over Prague

PETŘÍN LOOKOUT TOWER

Petřínská rozhledna; adult/child 50/40Kč; ⏱ 10am-10pm May, to 8pm Jun-Aug, to 7pm Apr & Sep, to 6pm Oct, to 5pm Sat & Sun Nov-Mar; Petřín funicular

Most long-time residents say the best views of Prague are from the top of this 62m-tall Eiffel Tower lookalike. While we prefer that near Strahov Monastery, we agree it's impressive to see the Central Bohemia forests on a clear day from here. The tower, which has 299 steps, was built in 1891 for the Prague Exposition.

PETŘÍN MIRROR MAZE

Bludiště; adult/child 40/30Kč; ☎ 10am-10pm May, to 8pm Jun-Aug, to 7pm Apr & Sep, to 6pm Oct, to 5pm Sat & Sun Nov-Mar; Petřín funicular

Also built for the 1891 Prague Exposition, this mirror maze isn't exactly cutting-edge, but it is good for a laugh, especially for kids. Adjacent is a diorama of a famous battle between Prazaks and invading Swedes on Charles Bridge in 1648.

SOUTH IN SMÍCHOV

Bordering Malá Strana, working-class Smíchov boasts several interesting sights and entertainment options. Home to *Brown-nosing* (2003) by David Černý (see p23), the **Futura Gallery** (☎ 251 511 804; www.futuraproject.cz; Holečkova 49; admission free; ⏰ 11am-6pm Wed-Sun; 🚋 176 to Holečkova) offers the unique 'opportunity' to stick your head inside the bum of a huge, bent-over statue. **Futurum** (☎ 257 328 571; www.musicbar.cz; Zborovská 7; cover 100Kč; ⏰ 9pm-3.30am; 🚋 4, 7, 10, 14 to Zborovská, night tram 54, 57, 58, 59 from Anděl) is a popular club, best known for its '80s and '90s video parties on Friday and Saturday nights.

Švandovo divadlo (☎ 234 651 111; www.svandovodivadlo.cz; Štefánikova 57; 🚋 6, 9, 12, 20 to Švandovo Divadlo) has lots of physical performances and plays often subtitled in English. There are summer classical concerts in the small **Mozart Museum** (☎ 257 317 465; www.bertramka.com; Vila Bertramka, Mozartova 169; tickets 390-450Kč; 🚋 4, 7, 9, 10 to Bertramka).

Neighbourhood eating and shopping includes:

Corleone (☎ 251 511 244; Na Bělidle 42; ⏰ 11am-11pm; Ⓜ Anděl) Tasty wood-fired pizza.

Na Verandách (Staropramen Brewery; ☎ 257 191 200; www.pivovarystaropramen.cz; Nádražní 84; ⏰ 11am-midnight; Ⓜ Anděl) Steins of Staropramen and quality pub grub.

Nový smíchov (☎ 257 284 111; Plzeňská 8; ⏰ 7am-midnight; Ⓜ Anděl) Staff sometimes Rollerblade between the aisles of this mall's agoraphobia-inducing Tesco hypermarket.

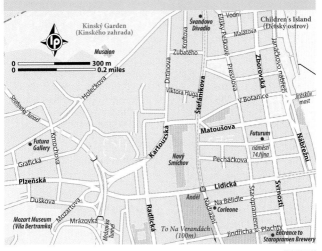

NEIGHBOURHOODS

MALÁ STRANA

⊙ PETŘÍN (ŠTEFANIK) OBSERVATORY

Štefánikova hvězdárna; ☎ 257 320 540; www.observatory.cz; adult/child 40/30Kč; ⏰ times vary according to season; Petřín funicular

Its odd opening hours (check the website) mean you have to plan ahead if you want to visit this 1920s 'people's observatory', which boasts a double Zeiss astrograph telescope for observation of the sun or the night sky.

Send an SMS to David Černý's 'Piss' sculpture

⊙ 'PISS' SCULPTURE

Proudy; Hergetova Cihelná, in front of the Kafka Museum; Ⓜ Malostranská

Cries of disbelief, laughter and raised cameras greet this saucy animatronic sculpture of two guys pissing in a puddle shaped like the Czech Republic. However, you can have even more fun with *Proudy* (2004) by David Černý. The microchip-controlled sculptures are writing out famous Prague literary quotations. Send an SMS to ☎ +420 724 370 770 and they'll pause mid-flow to spell out your message instead.

⊙ 'QUO VADIS' SCULPTURE

Behind the German Embassy, Vlašská 19; 🚋 12, 20, 22, 23 to Malostranské náměstí

Not strictly a public monument, this golden Trabant car on four legs is a David Černý tribute to 4000 East Germans who occupied the garden of the then West German Embassy in 1989, before being granted political asylum and leaving their Trabants behind. Today's German embassy is happy for you to peer through its back fence at the sculpture. Continue uphill along Vlašská, turn left into a children's park, and left again to find it.

⊙ WALLENSTEIN GARDEN

Valdštejnská zahrada; Letenská 10; admission free; ⏰ 10am-6pm Apr-Oct; Ⓜ Malostranská

Pop into Manufaktura for some retail therapy

One of Prague's tucked-away treasures (see also p18), this world of formal lawns, fountains, ponds and statues makes a perfect pit-stop en route to or from Prague castle. There are entrances via the Wallenstein Palace and from Leten-ská, but for that true through-the-looking-glass experience take the gate beside Malostranská metro station. Turn left from the escala-tors and then right on the steps.

There are several Manufaktura outlets across town, but this small branch right near Charles Bridge seems to keep its trim inven-tory especially enticing. You'll find great Czech wooden toys, beautiful-looking (if extremely chewy) honey gingerbread made from elaborate medieval moulds, and seasonal gifts like charming hand-painted Easter eggs. The branch up the hill at Nerudova 31 specialises in cosmetics.

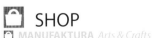 SHOP

MANUFAKTURA *Arts & Crafts*
☎ 257 533 678; www.manufaktura.biz; Mostecká 17; ⏱ 10am-7pm; Ⓜ Malos-transká or 🚋 12, 20, 22, 23 to Malostran-ské náměstí

MATERIAL *Glassware*
☎ 257 530 046; www.i-material.com; U lužického semináře 7; ⏱ 10.30am-9pm; Ⓜ Malostranská or 🚋 12, 20, 22, 23 to Malostranské náměstí

Material puts a modern twist on the Czech crystal industry, with its oversized contemporary vases, bowls and Dale Chihuly–like ornaments, candleholders, chandeliers and glasses. The firm boasts its 'drunken sailor' glass is spill-proof. Yet, despite well-spaced displays, it's a store where you immediately fear breaking something – and when you check the prices you realise you should!

PAVLA & OLGA *Fashion*
☎ 728 939 872; Vlašská 13; ☻ 2-7pm Mon-Fri, 3-7pm Sat; 🚋 12, 20, 22, 23 to Malostranské náměstí

Quirky-yet-fashionable clothes and hats are the handiwork of two sisters who originally were costume designers in the film and TV industry. Past customers include photographer Helmut Newton, Britpop band Blur and Czech supermodel Tereza Maxová, although they probably didn't shop in this tiny store. There's a larger branch at No 30 Karolíny Světlé (see p84).

🍴 EAT

🍴 BAR BAR
International $-$$
☎ 257 312 246; Všehrdova 17; ☻ noon-midnight Sun-Thu, to 2am Fri & Sat; 🚋 6, 9, 12, 20, 22, 23 to Újezd

This cosy, friendly cellar bar has a bohemian feel with its mix of antiques and contemporary arty touches, plus one of the most interesting menus in town. Delicious food runs the gamut from home-made Italian risotto and French crepes to Ukrainian *vareniky* (pasta-style parcels) and crème brûlée, plus there are excellent-value 100Kč daily menus.

🍴 BOHEMIA BAGEL *Café* $
☎ 257 310 694; Újezd 18; ☻ 7am-midnight Mon-Fri, 8am-midnight Sat & Sun; 🚋 6, 9, 12, 20, 22, 23 to Újezd

Not everyone still rates this one-time backpackers' favourite and internet café, but it's OK for quick snacks and all-American breakfasts. There's a Staré Město branch, too (p85).

🍴 CAFÉ SAVOY *Café* $-$$$
☎ 257 311 562; www.ambi.cz; Vítězná 5; ☻ 8am-10.30pm Mon-Fri, 9am-10.30pm Sat & Sun; 🚋 6, 9, 12, 20, 22, 23 to Újezd; ✗

Since its 2005 restoration, this gorgeous coffeehouse is becoming increasingly popular. Come for the stunning interior, brilliant breakfasts, Czech and French specialities, tasty coffees and good wine list. The pea soup (115Kč) is delicious and filling but, then again, you could always blow the budget on the 3463Kč (€125) caviar from the gourmet menu. Evening bookings advisable.

Watch the world pass by on Nerudova (p59)

COWBOYS
International $$$

☎ 296 826 107; Nerudova 40; ⊙ noon-2am; ⊛ 12, 20, 22, 23 to Malostranské náměstí

There's a fine line between chic and kitsch, but this upmarket steakhouse manages to stay on the right side of it, even in clunky boots and slightly tacky staff outfits. Its Dolce and Gabbana–style cowhide seats and adult-orientated rock soundtrack is offset with lots of soft lighting, exposed brick and a simple but deftly executed menu. There are succulent steaks and tasty fish, plus pasta and Portobello mushroom burger for nonmeat eaters.

The outdoor terrace, 70 steps up, overlooks Prague's rooftops.

CUKRKÁVALIMONÁDA
Café $-$$

☎ 257 530 628; Lázeňská 7; ⊙ 9am-6pm; ⊛ 12, 20, 22, 23 to Malostranské náměstí; Ⓥ ✗

This 20-seat gem is as sweet as its name, 'sugar-coffee-lemonade' (which is also the Czech equivalent of eeny meeny miny moe). The floral pattern on its historic ceiling beams caps an otherwise fairly bare wooden interior, while the blackboard menu offers delicious pasta, pancakes, salads, wines and cakes. (Eggs and omelettes aren't so good.) The 'superior' hot chocolate of 70% melted dark chocolate is positively primordial; apparently some even manage to finish it.

🍴 GITANES
Balkan/Mediterranean $$

☎ 257 530 163; www.gitanes.cz; Tržiště 7; ⏲ 11am-11.30pm; 🚊 12, 20, 22, 23 to Malostranské náměstí

This folksy-looking restaurant – think arched ceiling and lots of patterned tablecloths, paintings of rural idylls and wall hangings – is popular for its meat and seafood grills. The choice for vegetarians is a bit slim, even among the pasta section, but couples love to book its romantic private room.

🍴 HERGETOVA CIHELNÁ
International $$$

☎ 257 535 534; Cihelná 2b; ⏲ 9am-2am; Ⓜ Malostranská

Slightly less starry and more affordable than its sister, Kampa Park, this converted 18th-century *cihelná* (brickworks) is rated as a better bet by many locals, despite some recent grumbles about the consistency of its food. Hergetova Cihelná also boasts fantastic riverside views, while its menu includes pasta, fish, meat, Czech specialities and interesting 'top hat' food stacks. Ask for the cheaper wine list.

🍴 KAMPA PARK
International $$$$

☎ 257 532 685; Na Kampě 8b; ⏲ 11.30am-1am; 🚊 12, 20, 22, 23 to Malostranské náměstí

Prague's single most famous restaurant has been a celebrity-magnet since opening in 1994. Mick Jagger, Johnny Depp, Lauren Bacall, Robbie Williams and Bill and Hilary Clinton have all over-tipped the staff here, and it's where ordinary mortals go for a special evening. The modern international cuisine runs from spinach soufflé to Norwegian salmon with vanilla mash to veal filet mignon. However, it's the location that's truly stunning; from the riverside cobblestone terrace you overlook the lights of Charles Bridge. There's also a roof terrace and indoor dining room.

🍴 PÁLFFY PALÁC
French/International $$$-$$$$

☎ 257 530 522; Valdštejnská 14; ⏲ 11am-11pm; Ⓜ Malostranská

Dining by candlelight among the faded grandeur of the dining room, or perched on the 1st-floor terrace overlooking the palace gardens, is a truly memorable experience. Housed in the same neobaroque palace as the Prague Conservatoire, the Pálffy is popular for weekday lunches with staff from the nearby embassies and government offices.

🍴 RESTAURANT NEBOZÍZEK
International $$-$$$

☎ 257 315 329; Petřínské sady 411; 🕐 11am-11pm; 🚊 6, 9, 12, 20, 22, 23 to Újezd, then Petřín funicular

This 17th-century conservatory restaurant halfway up Petřín Hill now has a designer interior, with lots of pale Nordic furniture and Singapore orchids, as well as a menu that peppers its modern international menu with a few Czech staples. The views are fabulous, even if the place feels very touristy.

🍴 SQUARE *Mediterranean* $$$

☎ 257 532 109; Malostranské náměstí 5; 🕐 8am-1am Mon-Sat, to 9pm Sun; 🚊 12, 20, 22, 23 to Malostranské náměstí

Another outlet from the owners of Kampa Park, this follows much the same formula: take one slick, stylish interior and add upscale modern cuisine. Square has a tempting breakfast menu and better food than many in the vicinity. However, there are drawbacks, too. The very central location and transient trade makes it a bit soulless. Furthermore, our bill had 19% DPH (tax) added to the listed menu prices. The cheek.

🍴 U MALTÉZSKÝCH RYTÍŘŮ
Czech/International $$$

☎ 257 530 075; www.umaltezskychrytiru .cz; Prokopská 10; 🕐 1-11pm Mon-Sat, to 9pm Sun; 🚊 12, 20, 22, 23 to Malostranské náměstí

'At the Knights of Malta' is a romantic restaurant, serving top-notch and determinedly old-fashioned Czech cuisine like roast wild boar with rosehip sauce and duck breast in walnut sauce at candlelit tables under Gothic arches. Don't miss owner Nadia Černíková's legendary strudel. Book well ahead, too.

🍴 U MODRÉ KACHNIČKY
Czech $$$

☎ 257 320 308; Nebovidská 6; 🕐 noon-4pm & 6.30-11.30pm; 🚊 12, 20, 22, 23 to Hellichova or Újezd

A chintzy, baroque hunting lodge hidden away on a quiet side street, 'At the Blue Duckling' is a plush, old-fashioned place with quiet, candlelit nooks perfect for a romantic dinner. The menu is heavy on traditional Bohemian poultry, game and fish dishes.

🍴 U ZLATÉ STUDNĚ
International $$$$

☎ 257 533 322; U Zlaté studně 4; 🕐 noon-4pm & 6-11pm; Ⓜ Malostranská

Perched atop a Renaissance mansion within a champagne-cork's pop of the castle, 'At the Golden Well' enjoys one of the finest settings in Prague. Weather will dictate whether you sit in the red-and-gold dining room or head upstairs to the outdoor terrace – both command a stunning panorama. The menu demonstrates French, Mediterranean and Asian influences.

DRINK

▼ BARÁČNICKÁ RYCHTA *Pub*

☎ 257 532 461; Tržiště 23; ☽ noon-11.30pm Mon-Sat, 11.30-9pm Sun; ⛟ 12, 20, 22, 23 to Malostranské náměstí, night tram 57

Atmospherically tucked away behind Nerudova along a winding Malá Strana street, this 19th-century beer hall feels a bit furtive and secretive – at least for this neck of the woods. In the small upstairs bar you can sup four types of Svijanský beer as well as the more common Pilsner Urquell; food is also served. Downstairs, the larger Cabaret Hall hosts big bands and offbeat live gigs.

▼ BLUE LIGHT *Bar*

☎ 257 533 126; Josefská 1; ☽ 6pm-3am; ⛟ 12, 20, 22, 23 to Malostranské náměstí, night tram 57

The Blue Light is an appropriately dark and atmospheric jazz cavern, where you can enjoy a relaxed cocktail as you cast an eye over the vintage posters, records and graffiti that deck the walls. The background jazz is recorded rather than live, but on a quality sound system that never overpowers your conversation.

▼ MILL KAVÁRNA *Bar*

☎ 222 329 060; Kampa Park; ☽ noon-midnight; ⛟ 6, 9, 12, 20, 22, 23 to Újezd, night tram 57, 58, 59

This artists' café-bar in Kampa Park has existed in various guises since the communist era, but you might still hear it called Tato Kejkej, its most recent previous incarnation. One or two tourists are starting to find their way over the wooden footbridge beside the wooden mill wheel, but mainly it's local alternative types who fill the smoky, dimly lit interior, arriving for coffee, beer and the occasional live gig.

▼ ST NICHOLAS CAFÉ *Bar*

☎ 257 530 205; Tržiště 10; ☽ noon-1am Mon-Fri, 4pm-1am Sat & Sun; ⛟ 12, 20, 22, 23 to Malostranské náměstí, night tram 57

In the bustling heart of Malá Strana, this dark and peaceful Gothic cellar is in another world. Dimly lit alcoves, flickering candlelight and worn wooden tables make an appealing setting for a few quiet beers or a bottle of wine. (There are pizzas and salads on offer, but they're not particularly good.)

▼ U KOCOURA *Pub*

☎ 257 530 107; Nerudova 2; ☽ 11am-11pm; ⛟ 12, 20, 22, 23 to Malostranské náměstí

'The Tomcat' is a long-established traditional pub, still enjoying its reputation as a former favourite of ex-president Havel, and still managing to pull in a mostly Czech crowd despite being in the heart of tourist-ville (maybe it's the ever-present pall of cigarette smoke).

PLAY

☆ KLUB ÚJEZD Club
☎ 257 316 537; Újezd 18; ⏲ 2pm-4am; 🚋 6, 9, 12, 20, 22, 23 to Újezd, night tram 57, 58, 59

As interesting to visit as it is pronounce after a few beers, Klub Újezd (u-yez-d) is one of Prague's many 'alternative' bars, filled with a fascinating collection of handmade furniture and fittings, original art and weird wrought-iron sculptures. The three-floor venue progresses from a cellar DJ bar to a ground-floor pub and an upstairs café.

☆ POPOCAFÉPETL MUSIC CLUB Club
☎ 602 277 22; www.popocafépetl .cz; Újezd 19; ⏲ 4pm-2am, bands from 8.30pm; 🚋 6, 9, 12, 20, 22, 23 to Újezd, night tram 57, 58, 59

The latest branch of this popular minichain (see also p125) is a small club and live-music venue promising a deliberately eclectic mix: blues, Balkan, drum 'n' bass, ska, punk and more.

☆ U MALÉHO GLENA Bar/Club
☎ 257 531 717; www.malyglen.cz; Karmelitská 23; ⏲ 10am-2am, music from 9.30pm Sun-Thu, from 10pm Fri & Sat; 🚋 12, 20, 22, 23 to Malostranské náměstí, night tram 57

'Little Glen's' really is – little that is, so get here early. Yet it's the intimate size that makes this American-owned jazz/blues venue (and restaurant) so vital. Performers like Stan the Man put their heart and soul into entertaining an audience mere centimetres away. Amateurs are welcome at the regular jam sessions (as long as you're good!).

> STARÉ MĚSTO

Like a maze, Prague's Old Town is a place in which newcomers inevitably get lost. Lanes lead off side streets, alleys curve back on themselves, covered walkways obscure views. A steady stream of people flows constantly through the main tributaries, their footsteps echoing rhythmically along the cobblestone streets. But at some point you're

STARÉ MĚSTO

Please see over for map

bound to take a shortcut that turns into a very long cut and find you've come full circle.

In fact, disorientation is part of the joy of visiting this historic quarter. This is Kafka's home turf, encompassing the former Jewish Ghetto, its synagogues and cemetery. It's also home to the spiky-spired, Gothic Church of our Lady Before Týn and, yes, to *that* clock.

With the castle established in the 9th century, Prague's merchants set up shop across the river here in the 10th. Despite constant fears of flooding, and progressive building to raise its level, it's been the city's working heart ever since.

 # SEE

ASTRONOMICAL CLOCK

Old Town Hall, Staroměstské náměstí; 🕐 **chiming 9am-9pm;** Ⓜ **Staroměstská**
Ironically, if you wish to tell the time in the Old Town Sq, it's easier to look at the clock above this, because this 1490 mechanical marvel is tricky to decipher (see the boxed text, p74). The clock's creator, Master Hanuš, was allegedly blinded so he could not duplicate the clock elsewhere, although this is undoubtedly myth. See p14 for more on the Astronomical Clock.

BETHLEHEM CHAPEL

Betlémská kaple; ☎ **224 248 595; Betlémské náměstí 3; adult/child 40/20Kč;** 🕐 **9am-6.30pm Tue-Sun**

The Gothic spires of the Church of Our Lady Before Týn (p74) loom over the Old Town Sq

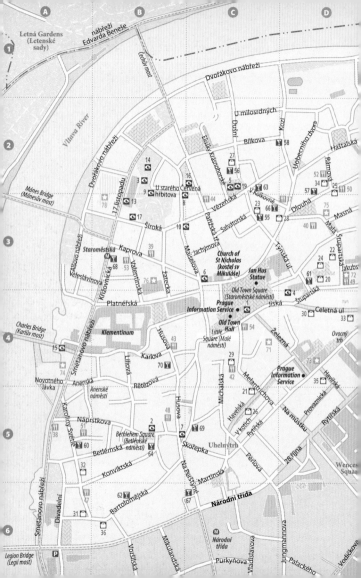

Letná Gardens
(Letenské
sady)

nábřeží
Edvarda Beneše

Vltava River

Dvořákovo nábřeží

U milosrdných

Bílkova

Haštalská

58

Mánes Bridge
(Mánesův most)

17 listopadu

Dvořákovo nábřeží

14

9 U starého Červená
   hřbitova

Elišky Krásnohorské

Pařížská třída

Vězeňská

Kozí

52 75
34
57

25
50

78

16

44

27
56

19

63

66
55

Rámová

Dlouhá

Masná

13

17

Široká

10

Jáchymova

Salvátorská

23

28

Masná

40

Malá Štupartská

Kaprova

39

Staroměstská

Alšovo nábřeží

68

Valentinská

76

Žatecká

Maiselova

6

Church of
St Nicholas
(kostel sv
Mikuláše)

Tynská ul

Jan Hus
Statue

24

22 Štupartská

61
20

Jakubská

72
49

Veleslavínova

Křížovnická

Smetanovo nábřeží

Charles Bridge
(Karlův most)

15

74

Novotného
lávka

Platnéřská

Klementinum

Husova

Anenská

Liliová

Karlova

70

Rětězová

Anénské
náměstí

Staroměstské
náměstí

Old Town Square
(Staroměstské náměstí)

Prague
Information Service

Old Town
Hall

Little
Square (Malé
náměstí)

Jilská

4

Michalská

29

42

Jiřská

30

Celetná ul

33

Ovocný
trh

73

35

Prague
Information
Service

Železná

54

Havelská

Provaznická

Karoliny Světlé

Náprstkova

38

60

Betlémské náměstí

Bethlehem Square
(Betlémské
náměstí)

2

7

48

Husova

Na Perštýně

32

Konviktská

54

Skořepka

69

Uhelný trh

21

26

V kotcích

Rytířská

Melantrichova

Na můstku

Perlova

28. října

Rytířská

Wences
Squar

Smetanovo nábřeží

Divadelní

31

62

36

Bartolomějská

Na Perštýně

67

Martinská

Voršilská

Mikulandská

Národní třída

Národní
třída

Vladislavova

Jungmannova

Purkyňova

Palackého

Vodičk

Legion Bridge
(Legií most)

P

Apr-Oct, to 5.30pm Tue-Sun Nov-Mar; M Národní Třída
Although a reconstruction, this barnlike church uses the pulpit and some original walls from the 3000-seater where the great Czech reformer Jan Hus preached from 1402 to 1412. Hus was burned at the stake for heresy in 1415, an anniversary commemorated every 5 July. One of the nicest things about the church, however, is that it brings you to a very pleasant quarter; the picturesque streets leading off Betlémské náměstí are a joy to explore.

🄲 CHURCH OF OUR LADY BEFORE TÝN

Kostel Panny Marie před Týnem; http://tynska.farnost.cz; Staroměstské náměstí; admission free; 🕙 services at 5pm Tue & Fri, 6pm Wed & Thu, 8am Sat, 9.30am & 9pm Sun; M Staroměstská
Its distinctively spiky Gothic spires make the Týn Church an unmistakable Old Town landmark. Straight out of a 15th-century, and probably slightly cruel, fairy tale, they rise up behind the four-storey Týn School that obscures the rest of the building. The church, housing the tomb of Tycho Brahe (see the boxed text, opposite), is only open for services (times change, so check the website) but you can always peer through the glass doors. The cobbled **Týnský dvůr** courtyard lies behind.

🄲 FRANZ KAFKA MONUMENT

www.franzkafka-soc.cz; Vězeňská; M Staroměstská
Jaroslav Róna's unusual sculpture of a mini-Franz sitting piggyback

TIME'S ARROW

Its upper disc is the only original element of Prague's Astronomical Clock. The figures of the Turk, Death, Greed and Vanity beside it were added in the 1800s. The figures of the 12 apostles, which appear hourly, and the lower calendar disc, with 12 monthly scenes of rural life by artist Josef Mánes, are both 19th-century additions.

The three hands on the upper face measure solar, lunar and stellar movements. The sun-hand points to the hour on the Roman-numeral ring; the top XII is noon and the bottom XII is midnight. The mini-sun on the same pointer traces a circle through the blue zone of day, the brown zone of dusk (Crepusculum in Latin) in the west (Occasus), the black vector of night, and dawn (Aurora) in the east (Ortus). From this, the hours of sunrise and sunset can be read.

Likewise, the moon-hands traces a path through day and night. The small moving ring in the middle of the face marks the zodiac, and the position of the mini-sun and mini-moon over it indicates which house of the zodiac each is in.

THE TRIALS OF TYCHO BRAHE

It's fair to describe Tycho Brahe, who's buried in Our Lady Before Týn, as something of a character. This Danish father of modern astronomy catalogued thousands of stars, made stunningly accurate observations in an era before telescopes, and helped his assistant Johannes Kepler derive the laws of planetary motion. He came to Prague in 1599 as Emperor Rudolf II's official mathematician.

But Brahe also dabbled in astrology and alchemy. He lost part of his nose in a duel and wore a metal replacement. His pet moose drank too much beer, fell down the stairs and died. In Prague, Brahe himself died in 1601 of a bladder infection, reputedly because he was too polite to go to the toilet during a long banquet. Only recently have historians decided he was probably poisoned instead.

on his own headless body was unveiled in 2003. Commissioned by Prague's Franz Kafka Society, it's beside the Spanish Synagogue.

⊙ FRANZ KAFKA'S BIRTHPLACE

Náměstí Franze Kafky 3;
M Staroměstská

An oft-photographed bust of the great writer marks the building where he was born on 3 July 1883, at what was then U Radnice 5. Now, this spot in the shadow of the Old Town Sq's Church of St

Nicholas is named after him. For more Kafka landmarks see p142.

⊙ 'HANGING OUT' SCULPTURE

Viselec; cnr Husova & Skořepka;
M Národní třída

Here's more inspired madness from artist David Černý (p23). Look up at this corner; you'll see a bearded, bespectacled chap not unlike Sigmund Freud casually dangling by one hand from a pole way above the street. In Czech the 1997 'Hanging Out' is called *Viselec*.

⊙ JEWISH TOWN HALL

Židovská radnice; M Staroměstská

Next to the Old-New Synagogue, this town hall was built by Jewish Ghetto mayor Mordechai Maisel in 1586. It's worth noting for its clock tower, which has one Hebrew face where the hands run 'backwards' like Hebrew script.

⊙ MUNICIPAL HOUSE

Obecní dům; ☎ 222 002 101; www .obecni-dum.cz; náměstí Republiky 5; guided tours 150Kč; ⏰ bldg 7.30am-11pm, information centre 10am-6pm, tours 2-4 times daily, see website; M Náměstí Republiky

This is what Czech-ness looks like. An Art Nouveau expression of national aspirations, Municipal House (see also p21) is laden with symbolism; the *Homage to Prague* mosaic above the entrance is set between sculptures representing the oppression and rebirth of the Czech people. Visit the café (p90), see a concert in Smetana Hall or take a tour. For individual travellers, these can only be booked on the same day from the information office to the left of the lobby stairs. In 2007 the administration was hoping to open the billiards room and a sweet shop.

MUSEUM OF CZECH CUBISM

Muzeum Českého kubismu; ☎ 224 301 003; House of the Black Madonna, Ovocný trh 19; adult/child 100/50Kč; 🕙 10am-6pm Tue-Sun; Ⓜ Náměstí Republiky

A proud reminder that the Czechs were the only people to apply cubist principles to architecture and furniture, Josef Gočlár's 1912 House of the Black Madonna – itself strikingly angular – has three floors of oddly shaped ceramics, glassware, paintings, chairs and sofas you wouldn't want to get into an argument with.

MUSEUM OF DECORATIVE ARTS

Umělecko-průmyslové muzeum; ☎ 251 093 111; www.upm.cz; 17.listopadu 2; combined entry with English audioguide adult/child 130/80Kč, without audioguide 120/70Kč, permanent collection with audioguide 90/50Kč, Tue 5-7pm

free; 🕙 10am-7pm Tue, to 6pm Wed-Sun; Ⓜ Staroměstská

It's a little musty and there are obvious potential improvements, but some of its individual displays alone warrant a visit to this museum. Through a barrel-vaulted staircase beautifully decorated with colourful ceramics, stained-glass and frescoes, you find four rooms of glass, ceramics (including Pavel Janák's cubist box), costumes, clocks, watches and a few precious Josef Sudek photographs. Pull out the drawers of book covers and posters in the fine graphic-arts section, and browse through the tempting shop.

OLD TOWN BRIDGE TOWER

Staroměstské mostecká vez; ☎ 224 220 569; adult/concession 50/40Kč; 🕙 10am-10pm Jun-Sep, to 7pm Apr, May, Oct, to 6pm Mar, to 5pm Nov-Feb

Blackened with age (but maybe up for renovation), this Gothic tower on the Staré Město side of Charles Bridge was one of Prague's original town fortifications. It's not only an appealing sight but also houses an observation tower with front-row views of the city's rooftops.

OLD-NEW SYNAGOGUE

Staronová synagóga; ☎ 224 819 456; Červená 2; adult/child 200/140Kč; 🕙 9.30am-5pm Sun-Thu, 9am-4pm Fri; Ⓜ Staroměstská

Students contemplate the weird and wonderful artwork in the Museum of Czech Cubism

With its steep roof, Gothic gables and descending entrance, this 13th-century synagogue is the source of the most famous golem legend (see the boxed text, p78). Europe's oldest working synagogue, it looks much as it would have five centuries ago. The pulpit is surrounded by a wrought-iron grill and on the eastern wall is the Holy Ark holding Torah scrolls.

POWDER GATE
Prašná brána; Na příkopě; adult/child 40/30Kč; 10am-6pm May-Oct; **M Náměstí Republiky**
Built in the 15th century over one of the Old Town's original 13 gates, the 65m Powder Gate derives its

name from its role as a gunpowder store in the 18th century. Given a neo-Gothic makeover 100 years later, its biggest attraction today is its outward appearance.

JEWISH MUSEUM
This **museum** (Židovské muzeum; 222 317 191; www.jewishmuseum.cz; adult/child 290/190Kč; 9am-6pm Sun-Fri Apr-Oct, to 4.30pm Sun-Fri Nov-Mar, closed on Jewish holidays; **M Staroměstská**) comprises the six sites listed in the following reviews. Tickets are sold at the Pinkas Synagogue, the Ceremonial Hall and the Spanish Synagogue; the Pinkas Synagogue has the longest queues, the Spanish Synagogue the shortest. There's

GOLEM CITY

Tales of golems, or servants created from clay, date back to early Judaism. However, the most famous such mythical creature belonged to 16th-century Prague's Rabbi Löw, of the Old-New Synagogue. Löw is said to have used mud from the Vltava's banks to create a golem to protect the Prague ghetto. However, left alone one Sabbath, the creature ran amok and Rabbi Löw was forced to rush out of a service and remove the magic talisman that kept it moving. He then carried the lifeless body into the synagogue's attic, where some insist it remains. In 1915, Gustav Meyrink's Austrian novel *Der Golem* reprised the story and brought it into the European mainstream.

also a 470/310Kč combined ticket to the Old-New Synagogue (p76). Men must cover their heads, so paper yarmulkes are provided at the entrances.

◉ KLAUS SYNAGOGUE & CEREMONIAL HALL

Klauzová synagóga & Obřadní Síň; U Starého hřbitova 1
Both the baroque Klaus Synagogue and the nearby Ceremonial Hall contain exhibits on Jewish ceremonies and other traditions, most interesting for the historian or devout visitor.

◉ MAISEL SYNAGOGUE

Maiselova synagóga; Maiselova 10
Mordechai Maisel was mayor of the Jewish ghetto under the liberal rule of Emperor Rudolf II during the 16th and 17th centuries. The synagogue with his name houses an exhibit of Czech Jewish history right up to emancipation in the 19th century.

◉ OLD JEWISH CEMETERY

Starý židovský hřbitov; entrance from Široká
The city authorities once insisted Jews were interred only here –

Wander through the Old Jewish Cemetery

GLIMPSE THE OLD JEWISH CEMETERY FOR FREE

If the rest of the Jewish Museum doesn't interest you, or you're feeling a bit impecunious, it's possible to steal a peek of the Old Jewish Cemetery's jumbled headstones through a back window of the Museum of Decorative Arts (see p76). You needn't pay admission to that museum, either. The relevant window is opposite the 1st-floor cloakroom, before tickets are checked. There is some meshing across the glass, but the view is fine (unless they read this and decide on curtains).

nowhere else – so by the time the 'garden of the dead' stopped taking new burials in 1787 it was full to bursting (see also p13). Today, you enter via the Pinkas Synagogue and exit near the Klaus Synagogue and Ceremonial Hall. Watch for the prominent graves near the main gate of Mordechai Maisel and Rabbi Löw, and be aware that conditions at this popular attraction sometimes feel almost as crowded for the living as among the dead. Since 1787 Jewish burials have been in Žižkov (p120).

PINKAS SYNAGOGUE
Pinkasova synagóga; Široká 3
Built in 1535, this was used for worship until 1941. Today it's a

moving Holocaust memorial, its walls inscribed with the names, birth dates, and dates of disappearance of 77,297 Czech Jews. Upstairs are drawings by children imprisoned during WWII in the Terezín concentration camp outside Prague.

SPANISH SYNAGOGUE
Španělská synagóga; Vězeňská 1
The most beautiful of the museum's synagogues, this boasts an ornate Moorish interior, an exhibition on recent Jewish history and a handy bookshop.

SHOP

ANAGRAM Books
☎ 224 895 737; www.anagram.cz; Týn 4; ⏰ 10am-8pm Mon-Sat, to 7pm Sun; Ⓜ Náměstí Republiky or Staroměstské
A good spot to look for Czech works in translation, this excellent English-language bookshop is a community-minded place that organises film evenings.

ART DÉCORATIF Arts & Crafts
☎ 224 222 283; Melantrichova 5; ⏰ 10am-8pm; Ⓜ Můstek
This is a beautiful shop dealing in Czech-made reproductions of fine Art Nouveau and Art Deco glassware, jewellery and fabrics, including some stunning vases and bowls.

🏠 BIG BEN *Books*

☎ 224 826 565; www.bigbenbookshop
.com; Malá Štupartská 5; 🕙 9am-6.30pm
Mon-Fri, 10am-5pm Sat, noon-5pm Sun;
Ⓜ Náměstí Republiky

A small but very well-stocked
English-language bookshop, Big
Ben also sells English-language
newspapers and magazines at the
counter.

🏠 BOHÈME *Fashion*

☎ 224 818 840; www.boheme.cz; Dušní
8; 🕙 11am-8pm Mon-Fri, to 5pm Sat;
Ⓜ Staroměstská

To say – truthfully – that knitwear
forms the basis of this collection
makes it sound less interesting
than it is. Designer Hana Stocklas-
sa has woven plastic black stripes
into grey vests, knitted sleeveless
turtlenecks, and added coarse-
stitched denim pieces to create an
overall preppy/fashionable look.
The shirts and jumpers discreetly

UNITED CZECH DESIGNERS

Bohème (above) and Klara Nademlýnská
(opposite) aren't the only original fashion designers selling their wares in Staré
Město. They belong to a group of eight
boutiques that have banded together
under the **Czech Fashion Centre** (www.
czechfashion.cz) marketing group. Pop
into one of the above and pick up a leaflet
with the names and a map of the rest.

---

embroidered with a Czech lion
make stylish souvenirs.

🏠 BOTANICUS *Cosmetics*

☎ 224 895 445; Týn 3; 🕙 10am-8pm;
Ⓜ Náměstí Republiky

Prepare for olfactory overload in
this popular old apothecary, which
sells natural health and beauty
products in slightly nostalgic
packaging. The scented soaps,
herbal bath oils and shampoos,
fruit cordials and handmade paper
products are made from herbs and
plants grown on an organic farm
east of Prague.

🏠 GRANÁT TURNOV *Jewellery*

☎ 222 315 612; www.granat-cz.com;
Dlouhá 28; 🕙 10am-6pm Mon-Fri,
to 1pm Sat; Ⓜ Náměstí Republiky or
Staroměstské

The vast array of stores selling garnet jewellery in Prague is confusing,
but this is the connoisseurs' favourite and it's easy to see why. As the
largest national manufacturer, it
has a huge range, from genuine
gold and garnet pieces to more
affordable gold-plated silver and
vltavín (or moldavite, a dark green
semiprecious stone). Look for the
sign 'Bohemian Garnet Jewellery'.

🏠 HAVELSKÁ MARKET
Arts & Crafts

Havelská; 🕙 7.30am-6pm Mon-Fri,
8.30am-6pm Sat & Sun; Ⓜ Můstek

Souvenirs have insinuated themselves among the fruit and veg of this formerly produce-only market. While the shops on either side of the street are selling entirely resistible tat, the market stalls are worth a quick browse for fresh honey or sweets, as well as colourfully painted eggs sold in the run-up to Easter.

🛒 KEBAB *Fashion*

☎ 224 818 840; www.kebabstore.com; Dušní 13; ⏲ 10am-8pm Mon-Fri, noon-6pm Sat; Ⓜ Staroměstská
The coolest streetwear boutique in Prague is notable for its stylish but humorous interior, courtesy of designer Maxim Velčoský (creator of the famous

'Pure' barcoded ceramic tumbler resembling disposable plastic cups). Quirkily customised animal trophies are joined by a shelving area resembling laundromat washing machines, saucy retro beach scenes adorn the curtains of the changing rooms and much more. Clothes by young Czech designers sit alongside brands from Spain, France, Germany and the UK and US.

🛒 KLARA NADEMLÝNSKÁ *Fashion*

☎ 224 818 769; www.klaranademlynska.cz; Dlouhá 3; ⏲ 10am-7pm Mon-Fri, 11am-6pm Sat; Ⓜ Staroměstská
While Nademlýnská's upmarket womens- and menswear is refined,

Shop for souvenirs at Havelská Market

elegant and beautifully tailored, she still clearly has a keen eye for the latest global trends, which keeps her collections fresh and vital. Original pieces here cost as much as top-end high-street clothes in Western Europe.

◳ KUBISTA *Arts & Crafts*
☎ 224 214 852; www.kubista.cz; Celetná 12; ☷ 10am-6pm Tue-Sun; Ⓜ Náměstí Republiky

Even for fans of the cubist style, this museum shop feels slightly austere and intimidating. It's all so artfully arranged, you feel scared to touch anything. Still, if you're interested in further exploring cubist buildings in Prague its pocket-sized guides are invaluable.

◳ MANUFAKTURA *Arts & Crafts*
☎ 221 632 480; www.manufaktura.biz; Melantrichova 17; ☷ 10am-7.30pm; Ⓜ Můstek

The largest of eight Manufaktura stores across town (including at the airport), this is an emporium of Czech traditional crafts, with wooden toys, scented soaps, beeswax candles, ceramics, 'blue' printed fabrics, Bohemian lacework and more.

◳ MODERNISTA *Arts & Crafts*
☎ 224 214 852; www.modernista.cz; Celetná 12; ☷ 11am-7pm; Ⓜ Náměstí Republiky

This classy showcase of Czech cubism, Art Deco and similar design features covetable but reasonably affordable ceramics, jewellery, posters and books, with some furniture. Early-20th-century reproductions include cubist boxes (Pavel Janák), expressionist ashtrays (Vlastislav Hofman), wooden toys (Ladislav Sutnar) and Jindrich Halabala's iconic 1931 reclining armchair. Contemporary items like sperm-shaped teaspoons, 'Pure' cups (a bar-coded, porcelain version of disposable plastic cups) and Škoda toy cars add humour. Plans are in place to open the basement, turning the place into a huge temple to 20th- and 21st-century Czech design.

◳ POHÁDKA *Toys*
☎ 224 239 469; www.czechtoys.cz; Celetná 32; ☷ 9am-8pm; Ⓜ Náměstí Republiky

This store is sometimes beset by souvenir-hunting tour groups and it harbours *matryoshky* (Russian stacking dolls) – artefacts that have nothing to do with Prague, despite their annoying ubiquity. Surprisingly then, it's also a pretty good place to shop for genuine Czech toys, from cuddly Little Moles to marionettes, via costumed dolls, finger puppets, rocking horses, toy cars and more.

Janek Jaros
Owner of Modernista (opposite) & specialist in 20th-century Czech design

Prague's the only city on earth with cubist architecture. Why did this style so appeal to Czechs? Early-20th-century Prague was charming but provincial and a new generation of artists wanted to do more than just emulate the modern art emerging in France. Young painters and sculptors socialised with architects and designers, and their ideas bounced off one another. **Isn't it just a wacky curiosity?** The cubist style in architecture remains unique. However, Czech artist Pavel Janák's ceramic designs greatly influenced the Art Deco style. He was one of the first to use zigzag patterns. **Iconic pieces?** Janák's crystalline ceramic box sums up the movement. There's only one surviving original – in the Museum of Decorative Arts (p76). **What's your favourite?** Emil Králíček's lamppost (p97). It's not just the lamp-post but the whole setting – in the middle of the busiest Prague district and still completely hidden away. **Anything else to see?** The Museum of Czech Cubism (p76) and the cubist houses below Vyšehrad.

EXPLORE KAROLÍNY SVĚTLÉ

Toalette (below) is the perfect entrée to Karolíny Světlé, but it's not the only interesting stop on this narrow, snaking street. Several independent young designers, scurrilous bars and arty cafés all line the way between Náprstkova and Národní třída. Granted, the street can't really compete with its big-city counterparts, but it's got character and provides some respite from Prague's neon-lit shopping malls. As well as Toalette and Duende (p89), look out for the following:

Kabul (☎ 224 235 452; www.kabulrestaurant.cz; Karolíny Světlé 14; ✆ 11am-11pm) Delightful Afghan restaurant; courtyard out back.

Nábytek ProByt (☎ 224 235 452; Krocínova 5, cnr of Karolíny Světlé) Interesting homewares store.

Pavla & Olga (30 Karolíny Světlé; ✆ 10am-7pm) Design boutique; see p64.

🏛 QUBUS Arts & Crafts
☎ 222 313 151; www.qubus.cz; Rámová 3; ✆ 10am-6pm Mon-Fri; Ⓜ Staroměstská

This small shop looks more enticing online than in reality, but Qubus, run by leading designers Maxim Velčoský and Jakob Berdych, is an important Czech firm well worth knowing about. If you're taken by the idea of ceramic *matryoshky*, cake-slice-shaped candleholders, wine glasses resembling throwaway plastic cups, liquid lights and Lomo cameras, nip in here.

🏛 SPARKYS Toys
☎ 224 239 309; Havířská 2; 10am-7pm Mon-Sat, to 6pm Sun; Ⓜ Můstek

While this is Prague's biggest toy store and hard to miss, it seems firmly aimed at local residents. All the same, you can find traditional toys and marionettes among its

collection of teddy bears and DVDs. Enjoy the browse or ask a shop assistant.

🏛 TOALETTE Fashion
Karolíny Světlé 9; ✆ 10am-7pm Mon-Thu, to 6pm Fri, noon-4pm Sat; Ⓜ Národní Třída

Urban 20-somethings in particular will be delighted by these carefully selected secondhand clothes and accessories, which still have plenty of fashionable mileage in them. Some new designs are found on the dressmakers' dummies on the shopfloor.

🍴 EAT

🍴 BAKESHOP PRAHA Café $-$$
☎ 222 329 060; Kozí 1; ✆ 7am-7pm; Ⓜ Staroměstská; Ⓥ

Despite the name, this isn't just a bakery; an assortment of fresh Mediterranean salads, thick and healthy sandwiches, savoury pies and frothy cappuccinos are also offered to take away or eat in. While you wait for your quiche to be conventionally heated (no microwaves here, thank you), admire the artfully iced cakes – which taste as good as they look.

BELLEVUE French $$$$
☎ 224 221 443; www.zatisigroup.cz; Smetanovo náb 18; ⏰ noon-3pm & 5.30-11pm; 🚊 17, 18 to Karlovy lázně; V

Book a table on the terrace of this formal establishment, and come to enjoy the fabulous views of the river and castle, while tucking into gourmet cuisine. Revamped in 2006, Bellevue now offers a Eurasian choice of dishes from roasted veal lion in black truffle sauce to infused black cod on wasabi mash. The service, however, doesn't seem 100% revamped, so don't come on an evening when the odd blip might upset you.

BODEGUITA DEL MEDIO Cuban $$-$$$
☎ 224 813 922; Kaprova 5; ⏰ 10am-2am; M Staroměstská; V

A pleasant surprise. Not far from the Old Town Sq and accepting euros, this outreach of the famous Havana establishment doesn't look that promising. But once ensconced at a chunky wooden table

in the deliberately graffitied front room (or out the back or downstairs), diners will find the food good and zingy. Try the Creole bouillabaisse, gambas Punta Arenas (prawns with chilli, lime and ginger) or just a classic mojito cocktail.

BOHEMIA BAGEL Café $-$$
☎ 224 812 560; www.bohemiabagel .cz; Masná 2; ⏰ 7am-midnight Mon-Fri, 8am-midnight Sat & Sun; M Staroměstská; 🚼 V

When there were fewer choices in Prague, this expat establishment was more interesting. It still has its dedicated fans, who swear by the bagels, sandwiches, grills, American-style breakfasts and atmosphere. But with a more critical eye, the food looks a bit wilted, the toilets are sometimes scruffy and the internet access (2Kč a minute) is fairly pricey.

CASA ARGENTINA Latin American $$$
☎ 222 311 512; www.lacasaargen tina.cz; Dlouhá 35; ⏰ 10am-2am; M Náměstí Republiky

This relatively new place seems designed to tease Prague carnivores. The service is ditzy, the parilla-theme interior is kitsch, but the place serves such tasty grilled steaks that people find themselves returning, despite themselves. Local restaurant critics suggest you ask for your steak without butter and apply any sauce yourself.

🍴 COUNTRY LIFE *Vegetarian* $
☎ 224 213 366; Melantrichova 15; 🕑 9am-8.30pm Mon-Thu, to 6pm Fri, 11am-8.30pm Sun; Ⓜ Můstek

This veteran health-food outlet belongs to the old, hair-shirt veggie (in fact vegan) school. Its pay-by-weight buffet of salads, tofu burgers and hot dishes is by no means gourmet, especially later in the day. However, it's ridiculously cheap and quite popular. There's an attached shop too.

🍴 CREMERIA MILANO *Café* $
☎ 224 811 010; Pařížská 20; Ⓜ Staroměstská

For very little money, make believe you're rich, by popping into this upscale café and grabbing some out-of-this-world Cream & Dream gelati – unrivalled in Prague. While here, don't forget to swoon over the cakes too. The original **Cream & Dream** (☎ 224 211 035; Husova 12) is still going strong, although it's on a thoroughfare that's even more ridiculously crowded in summer.

🍴 DAHAB
North African/Middle Eastern $$
☎ 224 827 375; Dlouhá 33; 🕑 restaurant 11am-3pm & 5pm-midnight, takeaway noon-1am Apr-Oct, 11am-3pm & 5pm-midnight Nov-Mar; Ⓜ Náměstí Republiky

If you're coming to Dahab, do it properly and spend time lounging in the dimly lit main restaurant, which is like a North African souk, scattered with oriental rugs and cushions. The menu encompasses the usual – couscous, *tajine* (meat and vegetable stew), lamb and chicken dishes, baklava and even hookahs (hubble-bubble pipes). The longer-hours takeaway isn't so salubrious.

🍴 DINITZ CAFÉ
International $$
☎ 222 313 308; Na poříčí 12; 🕑 9am-3am; Ⓜ Náměstí Republiky

This spacious Art Deco café takes you back to the swinging 1920s, with its classy retro décor and evening jazz bands, which pull in a mature crowd. Breakfast is served all day and the main menu is pretty decent, although from our experience the food errs a wee bit on the oily side.

🍴 KLUB ARCHITEKTŮ
International $$
☎ 224 401 214; Betlémské náměstí 5; 🕑 11.30am-11.30pm; Ⓜ Národní Třída

Trust an architects' society to combine a candlelit 12th-century cellar with exposed industrial ducting and modern metalwork…whatever, they're doing something right, as this place is always busy. The extensive menu caters for vegetarians and vegans as well as carnivores but, as in any place with a big menu, the daily specials are always a good idea.

🍴 LA PROVENCE
French $$$-$$$$

☎ 257 535 050; www.kampagroup .com; Malá Štupartská 9; ⏰ noon-midnight; Ⓜ Náměstí Republiky

With its dark-wood beams, cushion-strewn benches, tightly arranged tables, dim yellow lighting and shelves crammed with cooking implements, cosy La Provence makes a good fist of passing itself off as a French country kitchen. The menu matches the décor, ranging from *Boeuf*

bourguignon (beef and red wine stew) to *Lapin provencal* (rabbit in tarragon sauce) to *Cassoulet au confit du canard* (cassoulet with duck confit).

🍴 LARY FARY *International* $$$
☎ 222 320 154; www.laryfary.cz; Dlouhá 30; ⏰ 11am-midnight; Ⓜ Náměstí Republiky; Ⓥ ⊠

Essentially an upmarket theme restaurant, 'Hocus Pocus' is big on atmosphere with its varied Moroccan, Polynesian and 'romantic' rooms, but its food is just competent and its waiters a tad pushy. The signature 'skewer', a giant kebab dangling from an iron stand, is fun for carnivores; pasta

Musicians perform at Dinitz Café

TOP VIEWS OF THE OLD TOWN SQUARE

The food might not be brilliant atop **U Prince** (☎ 224 213 807; www.hotelu prince.cz; Staroměstské náměstí 29), but the bird's-eye view of the Old Town Sq is. Find its rooftop terrace by taking the lift at the back of the entrance hall to the top and climbing the stairs from there. No reservations are taken.

is preferable to the bland veggie version. Sushi and Czech staples are also served.

🍽 LEHKÁ HLAVA *Vegetarian* $$

☎ 222 220 665; www.lehkahlava.cz; Borsov 2/280; ☽ 11.30am-11.30pm Mon-Fri, noon-11.30pm Sat & Sun, snacks & drinks only 3.30-5pm; ♿ 17, 18 to Karlovy lázně; 👶 Ⓥ ✕

Despite some hippy talk of 'delighting your soul' and 'supporting your whole body', 'Clear Head' proves quite chic; it's easily our favourite Prague veggie. Set in a historic house down a side street, it has colourful walls, tables inlaid with clear marbles (faintly glowing ultraviolet) and projected videos. The international menu – Mexican, Japanese, tapas etc – lives up to the setting too. The place is small, however, so you might want to book.

🍽 ORANGE MOON *Asian* $$

☎ 222 325 119; www.orangemoon .cz; Rámová 5; ☽ 11.30am-11.30pm; Ⓜ Náměstí Republiky

Buddhist statues, oriental carved-wood panels, paper lanterns and warm, sunny colours make for a welcoming combination at this two-floor popular Asian restaurant. The menu is mostly Thai, with authentically spicy dishes. There are also some Indonesian, Burmese and Indian dishes, with both Singha beer and Pilsner Urquell to take the edge off that chilli burn.

🍽 SIAM-I-SAN *Thai* $$-$$$

☎ 224 814 099; Valentinská 11; ☽ 10am-midnight; Ⓜ Staroměstská; Ⓥ

Unusually tucked away behind the glassware boutique Arzenal, this upmarket Thai restaurant is also bedecked with some of local designer Boris Šípek's unusual creations, from the Medusa-heads chandeliers to the merely decorative displays of racked glasses behind the bar. The food is authentically spicy – really very spicy – but there's always coconut ice-cream and sorbet for dessert.

🍸 DRINK

There are no night trams directly through the Old Town, so you will have to walk from the main hubs at Lazarská or metro stops at Národní Třída or Náměstí Republiky.

☕ ALCOHOL BAR *Bar*
☎ 224 811 744; www.alcoholbar.cz;
Dušní 6; ⏰ 7pm-3am; Ⓜ Staroměstská
A booklike drinks menu that's
more than 80 pages long, a
selection of 400 cocktails, a glint-
ing display of rum, tequila and
whisky and a cigar humidor – this
New York–style bar wheels in a
reasonably sophisticated mix of
international and local guests.

☕ ALOHA WAVE LOUNGE *Bar*
☎ 724 055 704; Dušní 11; ⏰ 6pm-
2am Sun-Tue, to 4am Wed-Sat;
Ⓜ Staroměstská
Those with a penchant for Tiki-
style palm fronds and 1950s surf-
dude posters will love this small,
fun and laidback cocktail bar.

☕ BOMBAY COCKTAIL BAR *Bar*
☎ 222 328 400; Dlouhá 13; ⏰ 4pm-2am;
Ⓜ Staroměstská
This spacious central bar is always
going to be a little mainstream –
and a lot too loud! – for some
tastes, but it's such a ridiculously
popular meet-up spot, you probably should know where it is.
Reasonably strong cocktails fuel a
happy atmosphere and even a little
dancing. (No stag parties allowed.)

☕ CASA BLU *Bar*
☎ 224 818 270; Kozí 15; ⏰ 11am-
midnight Sun-Thu, to 2am Fri & Sat;
Ⓜ Staroměstská

This Latin American bar feels a
little secretive, and if the windows
on Kozí are covered over, just turn
the corner onto Bílkova to get in.
Inside, street signs in Spanish,
Aztec blankets and lots of tequila
create a cosy atmosphere. Get here
before 6pm to catch happy hour.

☕ DUENDE *Bar*
☎ 775 186 077; www.duende.cz;
Karolíny Světlé 30'; ⏰ 11am-1am;
Ⓜ Národní Třída
Bedecked with intriguing photos
and all matter of quirky ephem-
era, this bohemian drinking den
attracts an arty, local crowd of
all ages. They come for a chat, a
glass of wine or to take in acoustic
music performances, from guitar
to violin.

☕ EBEL COFFEE HOUSE *Café*
☎ 224 895 788; Týn 2; ⏰ 9am-10pm;
Ⓜ Staroměstská
The 30 different sorts of coffee
aren't really as good as received
wisdom would have it, but this
courtyard café makes a charming bolthole to avoid the crowds
around the corner on the Old
Town Sq.

☕ FRIENDS *Bar*
☎ 224 211 920; Bartolomějská 11;
⏰ 8pm-6am; Ⓜ Národní Třída
Friends is a welcoming gay music-
and-video bar serving excellent

coffee, cocktails and wine. It's a good spot to sit back with a drink and check out the crowd, or join in the party spirit on assorted theme nights, which range from Czech pop music and movies to cowboy parties.

☎ GRAND CAFÉ ORIENT *Café*
☎ 224 224 240; www.grandcaféorient .cz; House of the Black Madonna, Ovocný trh 19; ☽ 9am-10pm Mon-Fri, 10am-10pm Sat & Sun; Ⓜ Náměstí Republiky
Cubism shines in this reborn gem. The 2005 refurbishment – after an 80-year closure – has followed Josef Gocar's original designs, with striking green cloth lampshades, striped green upholstery and an angular wooden bar and coathooks. The result is quite swish, and as popular with locals as it is with tourists.

☎ KONVIKT PUB *Pub*
☎ 224 231 971; Bartoloměsjká 11; ☽ 9am-midnight Mon-Fri, 11am-midnight Sat & Sun; Ⓜ Národní třída
If you're looking for a reasonably traditional, down-to-earth pub in Prague's historic centre, you could do a lot worse than the Konvikt. Set on a street filled with police offices, it serves good Pilsner Urquell and solid Bohemian fare.

☎ MARQUIS DE SADE *Bar*
☎ 224 817 505; Templová 8; ☽ 4pm-3am; Ⓜ Náměstí Republiky

Housed in a former First Republic bordello, this red-lined dive bar has a deliciously low-life feel. The ceiling is patched with a sheet, the floor is creaky and from the 'comfort' of the threadbare sofas, the upper gallery looks precarious. But first-timers, regular expats and local barflies all mingle over a beer, wine, absinth, Becherovka or Fernet shot in this determinedly cocktail-free zone.

☎ MUNICIPAL HOUSE CAFÉ *Café*
☎ 222 002 763; www.obecni-dum.cz; náměstí Republiky 5; ☽ 7.30am-11pm; Ⓜ Náměstí Republiky; ♿ Ⓥ
Everyone should visit this legendary Viennese-style coffeehouse at least once. With its opulent Secessionist fittings and its formally dressed staff, it certainly looks a picture, and it has historical import. As with any venue this well known, however, it feels a little restless in here. And the coffee is lousy. So whether it warrants returning too often is moot.

☎ TRETTERS *Bar*
☎ 224 811 165; www.tretters .cz; V Kolkovně 3; ☽ 7pm-3am; Ⓜ Staroměstská
If you're looking for a bar with flashy bar staff and some of Prague's besuited power brokers and beautiful people, start

TANKOVNA PUBS

For drinkers who don't like to stray too far from the source, the Pilsner brewery has been working with pubs and restaurants since 1995 to install large vertical storage tanks in their premises to keep unpasteurised beer fresh and especially flavoursome (rather than storing it in traditional kegs).

Among the first to serve such *tankova* beer were the upmarket 'pub reconstructions' **Kolkovna** (☎ 224 819 701; www.kolkovna.cz; V Kolkovně 8; ⏲ 11am-midnight) and **Celnice** (☎ 224 212 240; V Celnici 4; ⏲ 11am-midnight Sun-Thu, to 4am Fri & Sat).

The beer alone makes them both popular, although some customers will find them a bit too much like a designer's *idea* of a Czech pub. More old-fashioned *tankova* pubs include U Pinkasů (p113), U Rudolfina (below) and U Zlatého Tygra (p92).

with this 1930s New York–style cocktail bar, or head to sister bar **Ocean's Drive** (V Kolkovně 7) for a slightly more laidback Latin theme.

▼ U MEDVÍDKŮ *Pub*

☎ 224 211 916; Na Perštýně 7; ⏲ beer hall 11.30am-11pm, bar 4pm-3am; Ⓜ Národní Třída

At first glance the food is merely average and the oom-pah music flows as freely as the cheap Budvar beer. But 'At the Little Bear' has a few tricks up its sleeve. There's a 45-seat bar above – go to the very back and up the stairs. It also boasts two homebrews, Old Gott (delicious) and malty, 11.8% X-Beer (the strongest Czech *pivo*). Bottles of the first should be available in the beer hall. However, if low stocks mean otherwise, both are still usually available to go from the shop.

▼ U RUDOLFINA *Pub*

☎ 222 328 758; Křižovnická 10; ⏲ 11am-11pm; Ⓜ Staroměstská

A rare Old Town *pivnice* that doesn't woo tourists, but gets them, regardless. It's just that in the better, downstairs bar you might find more Czechs than usual. The waiters speak enough English and the food is quite decent. Our one reservation is that they're liable to charge more than they should. Check your bill or shrug it off as still cheap.

▼ U VEJVODŮ *Pub*

☎ 224 219 999; www.restaurace uvejvodu.cz; Jilská 4; ⏲ 10am-4am; Ⓜ Národní Třída

Like U Sudu (p113), this place is much larger than it initially seems, and has a cavernous rear. You only have to read the drinks menu to understand where beer tastes in Prague are heading. After Pilsner

Urquell, Gambrinus and Tmazý ležák dark beer, there's a non-alcoholic Radegast, Heineken, and Corona! The touristy menu keeps a traditional section, though, with pork knee cooked in that dark beer.

U ZLATÉHO TYGRA *Pub*
☎ 222 221 111; www.uzlatehotygra.cz; Husova 17; ⏰ 3-11pm; Ⓜ Staroměstská

It's all in the timing, or perhaps sheer luck, whether you find the 'Golden Tiger' full of tourists or having an authentic moment. Weekday evenings are often best. This was novelist Bohumil Hrabal's favourite drinking hole – there's a bust of him on the wall – and where Václav Havel took fellow president Bill Clinton in 1994 to show him a real Czech pub.

PLAY

AGHARTA JAZZ CENTRUM *Club*
☎ 222 211 275; www.agharta.cz; Železná 16; ⏰ 7pm-1am, music 9pm-midnight; Ⓜ Můstek

Agharta has been staging top-notch modern Czech jazz, blues, funk and fusion since 1991, but only moved into this very central

Soak up the atmosphere at the M1 Lounge

Old Town venue in 2004. A typical jazz cellar with red-brick vaults and a cosy bar and café, it hosts local and international artists. The centre also contains a music shop (open 7pm to midnight).

⭐ CHATEAU/L'ENFER ROUGE Club

☎ 222 316 328; www.chateaurouge .cz; Jakubská 2; ⏰ club 9pm-4am Mon-Thu, to 6am Fri-Sun, bar noon-3am Mon-Thu, to 4am Fri, 4pm-4am Sat & Sun; Ⓜ Náměstí Republiky

This long-term Prague institution has been going through something of a renaissance recently, partly driven by the 'urban' (hip hop, R&B, funky house, 'afrodisiak' etc) evenings in the red-walled, smoky L'Enfer Rouge club downstairs. Upstairs Chateau has more of a messy bar/pub atmosphere.

⭐ ESTATES THEATRE Concert Hall

Stavovské divadlo; ☎ 224 902 322; www.narodni-divadlo.cz; Ovocný trh; Ⓜ Můstek

This is the small but beautifully decorated theatre where Mozart premiered and personally conducted *Don Giovanni* on 29 October 1787. Although much of today's programme consists of second-rate Mozart homages – where you want to leave after

10 minutes – it is possible to see some good performances, including some ballets.

⭐ KARLOVY LÁZNĚ Club

☎ 222 220 502; www.karlovylazne.cz; Novotného lávka 1; admission 50-120Kč; ⏰ 9pm-5am; 🚋 17, 18 to Karlovy lázně

The self-proclaimed 'biggest club in the middle Europe' (sic) is a five-floor hive of heaving teenage bodies, full of alcohol and hormones. Different music on each floor – from urban, retro and disco to techno/drum'n'bass – might make it worth a one-off trip in a big, diverse group. However, it's hard to imagine too many repeat visits.

⭐ M1 LOUNGE Club

☎ 227 195 235; www.myspace.com/m1 lounge, www.m1lounge.com; Masná 1; admission free; ⏰ 10pm-4am Tue-Fri, 11pm-11am Sat; Ⓜ Staroměstská

A long, narrow tunnel of exposed concrete, where exposed air-con ducts and ultraviolet lighting contrast with candlelight and plush sofas, M1 attracts lots of English-speaking expats and well-heeled locals (no stag parties). Its flagship evening is Wednesday's mix of indie rock, Britpop and electro, although it's moving into after-party territory with Saturday night's funky 'Liquid Time'. (Pity about the single ladies' toilet, though. Did we miss something?)

⭐ RISE LOUTEK *Theatre*
☎ 222 324 568; www.riseloutek.cz; Žatecká 1; tickets 40Kč; 🕐 box office 3.30-6pm Wed & 1hr before performances, performances 2pm & 4pm Sat & Sun Oct-Apr; Ⓜ Staroměstská

Although it shares a building with the National Marionette Theatre, whose *Don Giovanni* you want to avoid, Rise Loutek is the real (sadly off-season) deal. Fairy stories, folk tales, variety shows and other one-hour shows are performed by hand puppets and marionettes. In Czech, but charming.

⭐ ROXY *Club*
☎ 224 826 296; www.roxy.cz; Dlouhá 33; cover 100-250Kč Fri & Sat, Mon free, other nights vary; 🕐 7pm-midnight Mon-Thu, to 6am Fri & Sat; Ⓜ Náměstí Republiky

In the shell of an Art Deco cinema, its ramshackle nature is an integral part of the treasured Roxy's charm. There's a lounge-lizard bar and 'experimental arts space' NoD upstairs, while a vaguely themed 'ice bar' (with tacky fibreglass polar bear and foosball) leads off the large main floor. DJs spin house, trance, chill-out and more. Live bands also

Chill out at the Roxy

play and free Mondays attracts droves of students.

☼ RUDOLFINUM *Concert Hall*
☎ 227 059 352; www.ceskafilharmonie
.cz; náměstí Jana Palacha 1; tickets 220-
600Kč; ⏰ box office 10am-6pm Mon-Fri;
Ⓜ Staroměstská

Despite a surprisingly small stage, the neo-Renaissance Rudolfinum's main Dvořák Hall has good acoustics and the cachet to attract internationally acclaimed troupes. Home to the Czech Philharmonic Orchestra, the venue's excellent reputation is also boosted by their sterling musicianship.

☼ SMETANA HALL *Concert Hall*
☎ 220 002 101; www.obecni-dum.cz;
Municipal House, náměstí Republiky 5;
tickets 250-600Kč; ⏰ box office 10am-
6pm; Ⓜ Náměstí Republiky

Acoustics? Who cares about slightly imperfect acoustics when a concert hall looks this good? Decorated with stunning ceiling murals, the 1200-seat Smetana Hall creates sufficient atmosphere on its own. House musicians the Prague Symphony Orchestra kick off the Prague Spring music festival (p27) here annually. Day-to-day performers are often less experienced.

> NOVÉ MĚSTO & VYŠEHRAD

Prague tour guides love to titillate their non-European customers with the fact that the city's Nové Město, or 'New' Town, was founded as long ago as 1348. Holy Roman Emperor Charles IV ordered it built to help transform his chosen imperial capital and, rather less grandly, because he fretted about fire risks and hygiene in cramped Staré Město.

The broad streets and boulevards thus constructed – including the horse market of Wenceslas Sq – laid the template for contemporary Prague's most Westernised district. The commercialism and touch of sleaze that's descended since 1989 merely add to this description.

NOVÉ MĚSTO & VYŠEHRAD

👁 SEE
Church of Our Lady of the Snows	1	D3
Cubist Lamppost	2	D2
Dancing Building	3	A6
Horse Sculpture	4	E3
Jan Palach Memorial	5	F4
Lucerna Passage	6	E4
Memorial to Victims of Communism	7	F4
Mucha Museum	8	E2
Museum of Communism	9	E2
National Museum	10	F4
Orthodox Cathedral of SS Cyril & Methodius	11	B6
Radio Free Europe Building	12	F4
Rašínovo Nábřeží 78	13	A6
Slav Island	14	A4
Wenceslas Square	15	E3
Wenceslas Statue	16	F4

🛍 SHOP
Bať a	17	D2
Cellarius	18	E3
Dům U Černé Růže	19	E2

Foto škoda	20	E3
Globe Bookshop & Café	21	B5
Helena Fejková Gallery	22	E3
Jan Pazdera	23	D4
Moser	(see 19)	
Palác Knih Neo Luxor	24	E3
Promod	25	D2
Slovanský Dům	26	E1
Tesco	27	C3

🍴 EAT
Banditos	28	E6
Café Louvre	29	C3
Hot	30	E3
Káva Káva Káva	31	C3
Kogo	32	E1
La Perle de Prague	(see 3)	
Legenda	33	F6
Lemon Leaf	34	B5
Modrý Zub	35	E2
Noodles	36	F3
Pizzeria Kmotra	37	B4
Sushi Point	38	E1
Universal	39	B4
Zahrada v Opeře	40	G4

🍸 DRINK
Jáma	41	D4
Kavárna Evropa	42	E3
Kavárna Lucerna	(see 4)	
Kavárna Slavia	43	A3
Novoměstský Pivovar	44	D4
Pivovarský Dům	45	D6
Tulip Café	46	B4
U Fleků	47	B4
U Pinkasů	48	D2
Vinárna U Sudu	49	D4

⭐ PLAY
Duplex	50	E3
Kino Světozor	51	E3
Laterna Magika	52	B3
Lucerna Music Bar	53	E3
Minor Theatre	54	D4
National Theatre	55	A3
Reduta Jazz Club	56	C3
State Opera	57	G4
Vagon	58	C3

Please see over for map

Crescent-shaped Nové Město is roped off from Staré Město by Národní třída, Na příkopě and Revoluční (although for simplicity, this guide lists those sights located just east of Revoluční in the Staré Město chapter).

In the south, Nové Město rubs up against the ruined citadel of Vyšehrad. According to myth, Princess Libuše prophesised a great city would rise here and married a ploughman called Přemysl to found its ruling dynasty. Even less fanciful historians agree this is one of Prague's founding settlements.

SEE

CHURCH OF OUR LADY OF THE SNOWS

Kostel Panny Marie Sněžné; Jungmannovo náměstí; 9am-6pm; **M Můstek**

Fenced in by other buildings, this unusual 14th-century church is easily overlooked, but shouldn't be. Charles IV planned it as Prague's largest church, but only its chancel was ever finished. So it's left seeming taller than it is long, with an Orthodox Christian–style mosaic over the door and an ornate black-and-gold altarpiece. Enter via the Austrian Cultural Institute (Österreiches Kulturforum).

CUBIST LAMPPOST

Jungmannovo náměstí; M Můstek

Angular but slightly chunky, made from striated concrete – the world's only cubist lamppost would be worth going out of the way to see. So it's a happy bonus this novelty is just around the corner from Wenceslas Sq.

DANCING BUILDING

Tančící dům; Rašínovo nábřeží 80; 17, 21 to Jiráskovo náměstí or **M Karlovo Náměstí**

Stroll along the riverfront to the gracefully twisting 'Dancing Building' by Bilbão Guggenheim creator Frank Gehry and local architect Vlado Milunič. Nicknamed

See the light at the world's only cubist lamppost

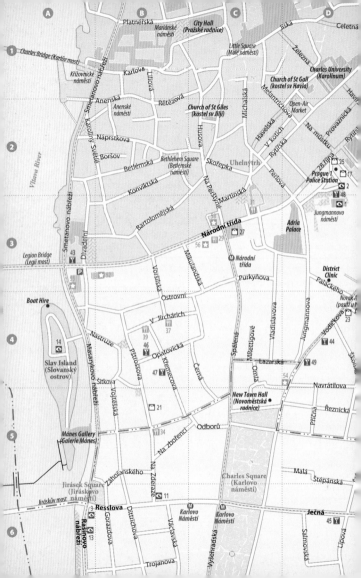

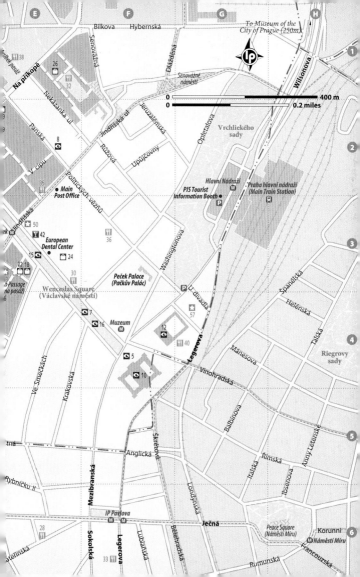

the 'Fred & Ginger Building' (after the legendary Fred Astaire and Ginger Rogers), this 1996 office is nipped in at the 'waist', to preserve neighbours' views, and has a top-floor restaurant, La Perle de Prague (p110). Nearby, humble **Rašínovo nábřeží 78** is what Václav Havel initially chose over Prague Castle as his presidential residence in 1989.

◯ JAN PALACH MEMORIAL

In front of the National Museum, Václavské náměstí; Ⓜ Muzeum
On 16 January 1969, university student Jan Palach set fire to himself and died in protest against the Soviet invasion of Czechoslovakia the preceding August. The exact spot the martyr fell is marked by a wooden cross in the pavement that seems to have suffered a small earthquake beneath it. The 16 January is now commemorated annually (see p26).

◯ LUCERNA PASSAGE

Lucerna pasáž; Štěpánská 61/Vodičkova 36; Ⓜ Můstek or Ⓣ 3, 9, 14 or 24 to Václavské náměstí
This 1920s Art Nouveau shopping arcade, running below the Lucerna Palace between Štěpánská and Vodičkova streets, was designed by ex-president Havel's grandfather, but is now better known for a café (p112), a club (p115) and the David Černý sculpture *Horse* (1999). Hanging from the atrium, this wry companion to the Wenceslas Sq statue has its Wenceslas (or Václav) astride the belly of a dead, upside-down steed. At least he's stopped short of flogging it.

MUCH ADO ABOUT MUCHA

Alfons Mucha (1860–1939) is the Czech answer to Austria's Gustav Klimt, England's William Morris or Scotland's Charles Rennie Mackintosh. One of the fathers – if not *the* father – of the global Art Nouveau movement, he allegedly started drawing before he could walk and found fame in Paris after producing a stunning poster for actress Sarah Bernhardt's 1895 play *Gismonda*.

A contract with Bernhardt, reams of advertising work and trips to America brought international renown. But this proud Czech returned home in 1909, where he designed the bank notes for 1918's First Republic and produced his opus, a collection of huge canvases entitled *Slav Epic*.

Mucha created the stunning interiors of Prague's Municipal House (p21) and designed a beautiful stained-glass window for St Vitus Cathedral (p49). In addition to the Mucha Museum (opposite), there are plans to bring his *Slav Epic* back from the provinces to Prague in 2008–09, hopefully in a new gallery in Holešovice.

MUCHA MUSEUM

☎ 221 451 333; www.mucha.cz; Panská 7; adult/student 120/60Kč; ⏰ 10am-6pm, to 5pm Nov-Mar; Ⓜ Můstek

Sensuous Slavic maidens and fin de siècle Parisian adverts line the walls of a gallery that will appeal more to existing Art Nouveau fans than potential converts. Although it's invaluable in putting his work into context, the 25-minute video on Mucha's life does drag a bit at the end, so revive yourself in the well-stocked shop.

MUSEUM OF COMMUNISM

Muzeum komunismu; ☎ 224 212 966; www.muzeumkomunismu; Na příkopě 10; adult/student 180/140Kč; child under 10yr free; ⏰ 9am-9pm; Ⓜ Můstek

Those attracted by the idea of this museum *might* enjoy it in practice, finding it part of the appeal that it reproduces the musty, down-at-heel style that characterised the period. However, the place is pretty shabby, really. Soviet pins, postcards and posters are on sale, but the section on the Velvet Revolution is rather thin.

MUSEUM OF THE CITY OF PRAGUE

Muzeum hlavního města Prahy; Map pp72-3, H2; ☎ 224 816 773; www.muzeumprahy.cz; Na poříčí 52; adult/student 80/30Kč; 1st Thu of month 1Kč; ⏰ 9am-6pm Tue-Sun, to 8pm 1st Thu of month; Ⓜ Florenc

ALL CHANGE AT THE NATIONAL MUSEUM

The hulking Národní muzeum was built in the 1880s as a symbol of Czech-ness, but more than 125 years later is a little unsteady on its foundations and needs a facelift. At the time of writing the museum building was due to close in late 2008, with its exhibits moving next door to the truly ugly Radio Free Europe building (p102). The entire collection will be housed here temporarily, before the museum gradually spreads back into its renovated original home and occupies both buildings.

To see how Prague looked before its walled Jewish ghetto was pulled down and St Vitus Cathedral was complete, pop along to see this museum's utterly charming model of the early-19th-century city. The model was an 11-year labour of love for its creator Antonín Langweil. Other displays cover Prague from prehistoric times to the 20th century.

NATIONAL MUSEUM

Národní muzeum; ☎ 224 497 111; www.nm.cz; Václavské náměstí; adult/child 100/50Kč, 1st Mon of month free; ⏰ 10am-6pm May-Sep, 9am-5pm Oct-Apr, closed 1st Tue of month; Ⓜ Muzeum

'An ugly, stuffy institution of the kind that gives national museums a bad name': so opined the UK's

Independent newspaper in 2006 and we half agree. Certainly the displays of rocks, fossils and stuffed animals are laughably old-fashioned. But the structure itself just needs a revamp, which it's getting (see p101). Fortunately, throughout the renovation, it should remain possible to do the exciting bits – look down Wenceslas Sq from the museum's front steps and visit the Jan Palach memorial below it.

● ORTHODOX CATHEDRAL OF SS CYRIL & METHODIUS

Kostel sv Cyril a Metodě; ☎ 224 920 686; Resslova 9, entrance on Na Zderaze; adult/child 50/20Kč; ⏱ 10am-5pm Tue-Sun May-Sep, to 4pm Tue-Sun Oct-Apr; Ⓜ Karlovo Náměstí

In 1942 seven Czech partisans involved in assassinating Reichs-protektor Reinhard Heydrich took refuge from the Nazis in this cathedral. Their tale is legendary (see the boxed text, below) and it's incredibly moving visiting the wreath-bedecked crypt where they resisted attempts to smoke and flood them out and then were either killed or took their own lives. Among multilingual explanations and bullet and shrapnel holes, you can see the Czechs' last desperate efforts to dig an escape route.

● RADIO FREE EUROPE BUILDING

Václavské náměstí; Ⓜ Muzeum
During the Cold War, US-financed Radio Free Europe was the most

SEVEN MEN AT DAYBREAK

During his short reign as the Nazi Reichsprotektor for Bohemia and Moravia, SS general Reinhard Heydrich earned himself the epithet 'the butcher of Prague'. He arrived in the Czech capital a chief architect of the Holocaust and Hitler's heir apparent and consolidated his reputation for arrogance by riding around the occupied city in an open-top Mercedes.

But installed in Czechoslovakia in 1941, the blonde, steely-blue-eyed Heydrich was dead by mid-1942, killed by resistance fighters trained in Britain.

The daring 'Operation Anthropoid' almost didn't succeed. When Jozef Gabčík stepped in front of Heydrich's slow-moving car on 27 May, his gun jammed. However, his compatriot Jan Kubiš lobbed a grenade, from which the German later died.

The assassins and five accomplices fled but were betrayed in their hiding place of SS Cyril & Methodius (above), where 750 German troops arrived at dawn on the 18 June. In the ensuing six-hour siege, three of the Czechs were killed and four committed suicide rather than surrender. In retribution for Heydrich's death, the Nazis unleashed a wave of terror, even razing the village of Lidice (since rebuilt).

For more, see Callum MacDonald's *The Killing of Reinhard Heydrich* (on sale in the cathedral), Alan Burgess's *Seven Men at Daybreak* or the 1975 film *Operation Daybreak*.

famous voice broadcasting from the capitalist West to the communist East. After 1989 it moved from Munich to Prague, into this former stock exchange and then communist parliament. In late 2008 the radio will be departing for Prague's outskirts, leaving this brutalist, 1970s glass-fronted building to the neighbouring National Museum.

☉ SLAV ISLAND
Slovanský ostrov; Masarykovo nábřezí; 🚋 6, 9,17, 18, 21, 22, 23 to Národní divaldo

If you simply must take to the Vltava River, you'll probably find it more fun to do so under your own steam, in a small boat, rather than on a larger cruise. Several places have rowboats, but on this leafy island you'll find both rowboats (75Kč per half hour) and pedalos (100Kč per half hour) for hire between April and October (depending on weather). No reservations are taken, but you'll need to present your passport or similar ID.

☉ WENCESLAS SQUARE
Václavské náměstí; Ⓜ Můstek or Muzeum

It's easy to be cynical about today's Wenceslas Sq (see also p16), with all its stag parties, persistent cabaret touts, drug dealers, pickpockets and garish advertising

Statue of St Wenceslas in Wenceslas Sq

VISITING VYŠEHRAD

Although it boasts a rotunda, casemates and more, a trip to Prague's second 'castle' of **Vyšehrad** (☎ 241 410 348; www.praha-vysehrad.cz; V Pevnosti 5; admission free; ☼ grounds 24hr; Ⓜ Vyšehrad) is pretty self-explanatory. Follow the signs from the metro and walk around this ruined citadel's magnificent **ramparts** for a stunning back-door view of the city. (The building with the eye-catching, swooping spires as you look north is the **Emmaus Monastery**; its original 14th-century spires were destroyed during WWII and replaced in the 1960s.) Elsewhere on the plateau is a beautiful **cemetery** (☼ 8am-4pm) and the **Church of SS Peter & Paul** (☎ 249 113 353; Krotunde 10; admission 30Kč; ☼ 9am-noon & 1-5pm Wed-Mon). For more details, visit the **information centre** (☼ 9.30am-6.30pm) by the main gate, and see p22.

There are some very average restaurants atop Vyšehrad; you're better off stopping at the following on your way back to Nové Město.

Oliva (☎ 222 520 288; www.olivarestaurant.cz; Plavecká 4; ☼ 11.30am-3pm & 6pm-midnight, family brunch 11am-4pm & 9pm-midnight Sat; ☎ 3, 7, 16, 17, 21 to Výtoň; ⚹ ✗) A midrange Mediterranean restaurant, well worth a detour for its pleasant decoration and menu of delicious but simply cooked fresh ingredients, including tomato tarte tatin starter, lamb shanks and warm chocolate gateau with pistachio cream.

Noodle bar (☎ 602 370 984; www.noodle.cz; Plavecká 4; ☼ noon-10pm Mon-Fri) Unimaginatively titled but imaginative weekday purveyor of simple Asian cuisine.

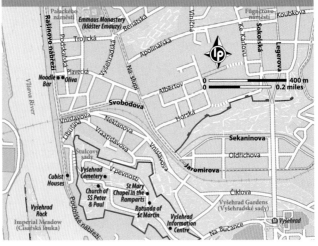

signs atop beautiful Art Nouveau buildings. That's progress, eh? However, the square that's seen so much momentous Czech history is still a pivotal hub, and its huge dimensions ensure a certain grandeur. Plans to refurbish it in upcoming years might see it regain more of its past splendour.

☉ WENCESLAS STATUE
sv Václav; Václavské náměstí;
M Muzeum

The focal point of Wenceslas Sq is this equestrian statue of St Wenceslas at its southern end. Sculptor Josef Myslbek has surrounded the 10th-century duke of Bohemia and the 'Good King Wenceslas' of Christmas carol fame (see the boxed text, p167) with four other patron saints of Bohemia – Prokop, Adalbert, Agnes, and Ludmila. Nearby another small **memorial to the victims of communism** displays photographs of Jan Palach and fellow martyred student Jan Zajíc.

SHOP

Intersecting Wenceslas Sq, and tracing the route that once ran around the Old Town, Na příkopě is one of Prague's most typical and reasonably fruitful shopping precincts. In the 19th century this fashionable street was the haunt of Austro-Hungarian café society. Today it's lined with all the usual high-street

suspects – Benetton, H&M, Mango and Zara – and dotted with the huge shopping malls that characterise the Prague retail experience, including dům U černé růže (House of the Black Rose) at No 12, Myslbek pasáž (www.myslbek.com) at No 21 and Slovanský dům at No 22 (p107).

☐ BAT'A *Shoes*
☎ 224 218 133; www.bata.com;
Václavské náměstí 6; ☽ 9am-9pm
Mon-Fri, to 7pm Sat, 10am-7pm Sun;
M Můstek

For generations, schoolchildren the world over have known Bata shoes (called Bat'a in the original). However, the Czech corporation's Wenceslas Sq store is a slightly more fashionable experience, incorporating cool streetwear brands alongside its own over six retail floors. A great Czech success story, the family-run firm has been going since 1894, and this 1929 flagship store is considered a Functionalist architectural masterpiece.

☐ CELLARIUS *Wine*
☎ 224 210 979; www.cellarius.cz;
Lucerna pasáž, Štěpánská 61/Vodičkova
36; ☽ 9.30am-9pm Mon-Sat, 3-8pm
Sun; M Můstek or ☖ 3, 9, 14 or 24 to
Václavské náměstí

Take a break from Czech beer and absinth; visit this cute vinotheque and sample Czech wine (eg a

Frankovka red or Müller Thurgau white) at its few outdoor seats.

📷 FOTO ŠKODA *Photography*
☎ 222 929 029; www.fotoskoda.cz; Vodičkova 37; 🕑 8.30am-8pm Mon-Fri, 9am-6pm Sat, mini-lab only noon-6.30pm Sun; Ⓜ Můstek

This excellent store provides all your photographic needs, from film, digital downloads and photo-CD burning to camera repairs, batteries and new equipment.

📷 HELENA FEJKOVÁ GALLERY *Fashion*
☎ 224 211 514; www.helenafejkova.cz; Lucerna pasáž, Štěpánská 61/Vodičkova 36; 🕑 10am-7pm Mon-Fri, to 3pm Sat; Ⓜ Můstek or 🚊 3, 9, 14 or 24 to Václavské náměstí

Fejková's designer clothes will appeal more to mature women, but females of all ages will enjoy the slightly Victorian showroom. Up the stairs opposite Kavarna Lucerna you'll find old shop dummies set between movie lights across a creaky floor. Some of the jewellery is quite funky and affordable.

📷 JAN PAZDERA *Photography*
☎ 224 216 197; Vodičkova 28; 🕑 10am-6pm Mon-Sat; Ⓜ Můstek or 🚊 3, 9, 14 or 24 to Václavské náměstí

Not so much for snap-happy holidaymakers (who should head

SCREEN BREAK
If rain spoils play during your break in Prague, don't worry. The list of things to do doesn't stop at drinking, riding trams and visiting museums. Cinemas in Prague usually show films in their original language, with Czech subtitles. So going to the movies is always feasible.

to Foto Škoda, left) as for serious photo enthusiasts, this has mesmerising displays of secondhand cameras, darkroom gear, lenses, binoculars and telescopes. Models range from the basic but sturdy Russian-made Zenit to expensive Leicas.

📷 MOSER *Glassware*
☎ 224 211 293; www.moser-glass.com; dům U černé růže, Na příkopě 12; 🕑 10am-8pm Mon-Fri, to 7pm Sat & Sun; Ⓜ Můstek

This exclusive Bohemian glass-maker was founded in Karlovy Vary in 1857 and is famous for its ornate designs – which here are housed in equally over-the-top, Gothic surrounds. For those preferring cleaner lines, one classic Moser design is Royal 9000, used in Prague Castle and UN headquarters in New York. Model 9009 (1500Kč apiece) is *the* ultimate old-fashioned champagne glass.

🏠 PALÁC KNIH NEO LUXOR
Books

☎ 221 111 336; Václavské náměstí 41;
🕑 8am-8pm Mon-Fri, 9am-7pm Sat,
10am-7pm Sun; Ⓜ Muzeum

Slightly musty though it is, Central Europe's largest bookstore is worth a browse, particularly for the wide basement selection of fiction and nonfiction in English, German, French and Russian, including Czech authors in translation. Elsewhere, there's internet access, a café and international newspapers.

🏠 PROMOD *Fashion*

☎ 296 327 700; Václavské náměstí 772/2; 🕑 10am-10pm Mon-Sat, 11am-7pm Sun; Ⓜ Můstek

French and other Continental readers, look away now; you'll be used to the delights this trendy young Gallic chain brings. However, American, Asian, Australian, British and Latin American travellers find this Czech branch a boon. Its range of affordable, covetable, up-to-the-minute fashion and jewellery might also be disposable, but it's a nice change from H&M.

🏠 SLOVANSKÝ DŮM
Department Store

☎ 221 451 400; www.slovanskydum.cz; Na příkopě 22; Ⓜ Náměstí Republiky

Even if you're totally uninterested in its fashion stores (from streetwise Miss Sixty to upmarket Cerruti via preppy Tommy Hilfiger), Prague's leading mall is worth knowing for its restaurants, including Kogo (p110) and its multiplex cinema. The complex was up for sale at the time of writing, but it's unlikely consumers will notice any difference.

🏠 TESCO *Department Store*

☎ 222 003 111; Národní třída 26;
🕑 8am-9pm Mon-Fri, 9am-8pm Sat,
10am-7pm Sun, supermarket 7am-10pm Mon-Fri, 8am-8pm Sat, 9am-8pm Sun;
Ⓜ Národní Třída

Right above the metro and beside one of the city's busiest tram stops, this five-storey monolith is no mere retail outlet. Oh, no. It's a cultural phenomenon, too, as all Prague expat life seems to sashay down its aisles at some point. Indeed, they all seem to be milling around the basement supermarket – together – whenever you have to dash for a few late-night supplies and find yourself behind a lengthy queue. The ground floor is good for last-minute toiletries, but terrible for last-minute umbrellas. (So flimsy! Try a *Bankrot* store on Wenceslas Sq instead.)

🍴 EAT

🍴 BANDITOS *Tex-Mex* $-$$

☎ 224 941 096; Melounova 2; 🕑 9am-12.30am Mon-Fri, noon-12.30am Sat, 5pm-midnight Sun; Ⓜ IP Pavlova

Smoke, loud chatter and heavy rock are the accompaniments to your meal in this wood-floored venue that's also popular with the suits who work at nearby Price-WaterhouseCoopers. Service can be slow, but the food is tasty, portions usually generous and there's a good range of artery-hardening, all-day breakfasts.

CAFÉ LOUVRE Café $
☎ 224 930 949; www.cafélouvre.cz; 1st fl, Národní třída 2; 8am-11.30pm Mon-Fri, 9am-11.30pm Sat & Sun; M Národní Třída;

Others are more famous, but French-style Louvre is arguably Prague's most amenable grand café. The atmosphere is wonderfully olde-worlde, but there's a proper nonsmoking section among its warren of rooms and it serves good coffee (a Prague rarity) as well as food. Pop in for a great breakfast before 11am, play a little billiards, and check out the associated art gallery downstairs when leaving.

GLOBE BOOKSHOP & CAFÉ Café $
☎ 224 934 203; Pštrossova 6; 10am-10pm; M Karlovo Náměstí

Mingle with expats at the Globe Bookshop & Café

Eat in Art Deco surrounds at Hot

Under new owners, this long-standing expat institution is looking good again, with its red café walls and quirky paintings. If you don't mind the Crackberry (sorry, Blackberry) and laptop owners treating it as their office, it does cheap-and-filling business lunches and American-style breakfasts, as well as dinners. Foremost, it's a bar, a place to mingle, post community ads or access the internet; its designation as a bookshop seems to be the least of it.

HOT *International* $$-$$$
☎ 222 247 240; Václavské náměstí 45;
🕑 7am-1am; Ⓜ Muzeum

This designer venue in the heart of the tourist maelstrom is like a supper-club for the new century, as a pretty upbeat, rocky soundtrack gradually kicks in over the evening. The renovated Art Deco space looks fantastic, with leather chairs and mood lighting up front, plus a swish 1960s sci-fi movie-set appearance at the rear. The pared-down menu offers either steaks (including fish) or pastas, but the food is rather good. Mysteriously, given the nightclub vibe, children under 12 eat free and there are regular 'Moravian evenings'.

SCOUT OUT SONA

No-one in Prague still uses the term 'SoNa' without irony, but the abbreviation coined by an American expat for the area *south of Národní* – and even leapt on by *Wallpaper** magazine as one of the world's 'hot 'hoods' – has stuck as a tongue-in-cheek description. It's never become as hip as pundits were forecasting at the start of the 21st century; it's even stagnated since all the fuss. However, if you want to explore, the following join the Globe (p108) and touristy U Fleků (p113) in the enclave between Národní třída, Spálená Myslíkova and the Vltava River:

Lemon Leaf (☎ 224 919 056; www.lemon.cz; Na Zderaze 14; 11am-11pm Mon-Thu, 11am-12.30am Fri, 12.30pm-12.30am Sat, 12.30-11pm Sun) One of the city's best Thai restaurants bizarrely dabbles in Italian too.

Pizzeria Kmotra (The Godmother; ☎ 224 934 100; V Jirchářích 12; 11am-midnight) Wood-fired margheritas to marinaras from one of Prague's oldest and busiest pizzerias.

Tulip Café (☎ 224 930 019; Opatovická 3; 11am-2am Sun-Thu, to 7am Fri-Sat) Service isn't great at this famous American expat hang-out and neither is the food, but it still pulls in customers for a drink.

Universal (☎ 224 934 416; www.universalrestaurant.cz; V Jirchářích 6; 11.30am-midnight) Comfy French-style bistro and bar, known for its Sunday buffet brunch.

🍴 KÁVA KÁVA KÁVA *Café* $

☎ 224 228 862; Platýz pasáž, Národní třída 37; 7am-10pm Mon-Fri, 9am-10pm Sat & Sun; Ⓜ Národní Třída

More people seem to come to this American-owned café tucked away in the Platýz courtyard for the wi-fi (charged for) and internet access downstairs than for the middling coffee. (It's won awards, but not from us.) It's a good spot for snacking, though, including unconventional bruschetta, served on black bread, and *medovník* (honey cake).

🍴 KOGO *Italian* $$-$$$$

☎ 221 451 259; Slovanský dům, Na příkopě 10; 9am-midnight; Ⓜ Náměstí Republiky; Ⓥ ⓑ

We find it quite amusing. Many residents complain this restaurant isn't as good as it used to be, but ask the same people for one reliable recommendation in Prague and they'll name this. Its secret is authentically Italian-style relaxed chic, but the top-notch pizza, pasta, steak, seafood and coffee don't hurt either. Although its shopping-mall location doesn't seem promising initially, there are courtyard tables in summer and high-chairs year-round for kids.

🍴 LA PERLE DE PRAGUE *French* $$$-$$$$

☎ 221 984 160; Rašínovo nábřeží 80; noon-2pm & 7-10.30pm Tue-Sat,

7-10.30pm Mon; 🚊 17, 21 to Jiráskovo náměstí or Ⓜ **Karlovo Náměstí**
On the 7th floor of the Dancing Building (p97), La Perle de Prague's outdoor terrace offers stunning views across the river to Prague Castle, as does its dining room to a lesser extent (smallish windows). Starchy, formal and very French, it's also very pricey. The two-course business lunch (490Kč) is the cheapest deal. Note to vegetarians: don't bother.

🍴 LEGENDA
Czech/International $
☎ 296 180 310; www.ilegenda.cz; Legerova 39; ⏱ 10.30am-midnight; Ⓜ **IP Pavlova**
This dark, buzzy place is repeatedly cited by travellers looking for a filling, functional feed – from Czech classics to pasta or steak. There's a 20Kč 'cover' charge and you'll pay for the bread unless you wave it away, but we guess that with generous portions at low prices these might be bearable inconveniences.

🍴 SUSHIPOINT
Japanese $$-$$$
☎ 222 211 013; www.sushi-point.cz; Myslbek pasáž, Na příkopě 19; ⏱ 11am-10pm; Ⓜ **Můstek**
There are more 'designed' sushi restaurants in Prague, and some cheaper. But although it's not particularly atmospherically located this is conveniently central and has food of a generally high standard. If you're the last customers to leave, being escorted by the kimono-clad waiter through a series of halls and back stairwells is a cinematic end to your evening.

🍴 ZAHRADA V OPEŘE
International $$$
☎ 224 239 685; www.zahradavopere .cz; Legerova 75; ⏱ 10am-10pm; Ⓜ **Muzeum**
This is one of those Prague surprises where rather than deteriorating into a tourist trap,

---

CHOPSTICKS AT DAWN
Looking for noodles in Nové Město? A cheap option is the modern, cheerfully decorated noodle bar **Modrý zub** (☎ 222 212 622; www.modryzub .com; Jindřišská 5; ⏱ 11am-11pm), although its cooking can be inconsistent. For a more upmarket experience, head to **Noodles** (☎ 234 100 100; www .hotel-yasmin.cz; Politických vězňů 12) in the Hotel Yasmin. Here the retro 1970s design includes large, furry blood-orange triffid-like sculptures, while the menu takes a very broad definition of noodles, listing Italian pasta alongside Indonesian *bami goreng*, Japanese *yaki udon* and even Mongolian *tsuivan* noodles. A further, cut-price restaurant, the Noodle bar (p104), is located further south en route to Vyšehrad.

the restaurant at the State Opera turns out to be a well-loved local gem, with a quirky but stylish interior. An interesting list of starters, including *Malsuka* (goat's cheese in Arabian pastry) and South African bobotie, precedes favourites like lamb fillets, salmon and nasi goreng.

DRINK

JÁMA *Bar*
☎ 224 222 383; V jámě 7; �) 11am-1am; Ⓜ Muzeum, night tram 55, 56, 58
This buzzing American expat bar and restaurant also attracts young Czechs with its leafy patio-cum-rear beer garden and mix of Pilsner Urquell, Gambrinus and Velkopopvický Kozel. Burgers, steaks, ribs and chicken wings are provided for the hungry.

KAVÁRNA EVROPA *Café*
☎ 224 228 117; Václavské náměstí 25; �) 9.30am-11pm; Ⓜ Můstek
Famed though it is, it's best just to peer through the window of this ornate Art Nouveau café on Wenceslas Sq and appreciate its fading grandeur from the pavement. Inside, it's a bit of a tourist trap.

KAVÁRNA LUCERNA *Café*
☎ 224 215 495; Lucerna pasáž, Štěpánská 61/Vodičkova 36; �) 10am-1am Mon-Sat, 11pm Sun; Ⓜ Můstek

or Ⓣ 3, 9, 14 or 24 to Václavské náměstí
A pre-cinema crowd joins card players, chain-smokers and bar-flies in this wonderfully atmospheric café, which nestles in an Art Nouveau shopping arcade where light filtered through the yellow cupola and dirty-coloured fake marble create an aura of bittersweet nostalgia. Chocolate cake or *mednovík* are pretty well the only non-liquid choices as you peer through the arched windows at David Černý's fibreglass *Horse*.

KAVÁRNA SLAVIA *Café*
☎ 224 220 957; www.caféslavia .cz; Národní třída 1; �) 8am-11pm; Ⓜ Národní Třída
The one-time hangout of Václav Havel and fellow anticommunist dissidents – and before them writers Rainer Maria Rilke and Franz Kafka – the Slavia now attracts locals and tourists equally. The revamped cherrywood and onyx interior still seems very 1970s, the food is average and the service is desultory. However if you bag a front table overlooking the castle, you'll forget such minor quibbles.

NOVOMĚSTSKÝ PIVOVAR *Pub*
☎ 224 232 448; www.npivovar.cz; Vodičkova 20; �) 8am-11.30pm Mon-Fri,

11.30am-11.30pm Sat, noon-10pm
Sun; M Můstek or 🚋 3, 9, 14, 24 to
Václavské náměstí

You realise this is going to be
another over-touristed *hospoda*
from the strains of oom-pah music
the moment the door opens. Con-
sequently, you'll be lucky to get
a table without a booking. Why
bother doing that? Well, the beer
is slightly cheaper than in similar
establishments and the food is not
merely edible but actually rather
decent.

Y PIVOVARSKÝ DŮM *Pub*
☎ 296 216 666; cnr Ječná & Lipová;
🕐 11am-11.30pm; 🚋 4, 6, 10, 16, 22,
23 to Štěpánská

Decked out with copper vats and
tiled floors, this microbrewery isn't
particularly Czech, although many
locals do take refuge here. The
main attraction is the flavoured
beers, including banana (the
nicest), coffee and blueberry.
Otherwise, stick to the own-brew
lager. We didn't find the food at all
outstanding, despite its reputation.

Y U FLEKŮ *Pub*
☎ 224 934 019; www.ufleku.cz;
Křemencova 11; 🕐 9am-11pm;
M Národní Třída or Karlovo Náměstí

Prague's oldest beer hall is like a
perpetual Oktoberfest, a warren
of drinking and dining rooms
clogged with rowdy tourists high

on oom-pah music and relatively pricey beer (59Kč for 0.4L).
Yet even those who dislike the
tavern's commercialisation find
themselves returning for its peerless 13-degree black 'Flek' lager.
Come in the morning for a little
quiet and note the Becherovka
liquor the waiters repeatedly offer
costs 79Kč a shot.

Y U PINKASŮ *Pub*
☎ 221 111 150; www.upinkasu.cz; Jungmannovo náměstí 16; 🕐 downstairs
10am-midnight, upstairs 11.30am-1am;
M Můstek

Allegedly Prague's oldest Pilsner
pub (1843), this was another
haunt of writer Bohumil Hrabal's
and it's a darn sight more local-
feeling (particularly upstairs)
than the more famous U zlatého
trygra. Also to its credit is that it's a
'tankovna' pub selling particularly
tasty unpasteurised Pilsner, which
is called *'hladinky'* by regulars.

Y VINÁRNA U SUDU *Bar*
☎ 222 232 207; www.usudu.cz; Vodičkova
10; 🕐 8am-3am Mon-Thu, to 4am Fri &
Sat, to 2am Sun; M Můstek or 🚋 3, 9,14,
24 to Lazarská, night tram 51-58

The small demure winebar
through the front door gives way
to an enormous underground
warren of seven different dimly
lit cellar bars and lounge spaces.
Increasingly legendary among

Irena Markovic
Photographer and keen clubber

What's the best thing about Prague clubbing? Clubs and pubs don't clo at 11pm or 2am, like in some other countries. Usually my friends and I stay out until 4am or 5am and try to go to at least two clubs. **Is it a 'cool' scene or a fun one?** It doesn't compare to other European cities, like Berlin, Paris or London, but Czech people love going out. Weekends are always crowde and you can't miss the fun. **We believe you're a big fan of the club M1 (p93). Why?** Great atmosphere. Slightly industrial décor, in a positive way, and I love the music they play. **And where to for some sophistication?** Ocean's Drive [see Tretters, p90]. They serve a great champagne. **Do you u derstand the '80s and '90s nights phenomenon?** No! Lucerna [opposite and Futurum (p61) have been playing this music for many years and I gues people like going because it's familiar and comfortable.

young expats and travellers, but still also popular with Czechs.

⭐ PLAY

✪ DUPLEX Club

☎ 224 232 319; www.duplexduplex.cz; Václavské náměstí 21; cover 300Kč; ⏱ 11pm-5am Wed-Sat; Ⓜ Můstek, night tram 55, 56, 58

Located in a glass cube perched on the 6th and 7th floors above Wenceslas Sq, this opulently decorated club has great views over the city and a penchant for trancey house music. Hosting a range of so-called MTV parties, Dirty Dancing and Bohemian eves, its central location attracts numerous stag parties.

✪ KINO SVĚTOZOR Cinema

☎ 224 946 824; www.kinosvetozor.cz; Vodičkova 41; tickets 80-100Kč; ⏱ screenings from 11am; Ⓜ Můstek or Ⓣ 3, 9, 14 or 24 to Václavské náměstí

Světozor is the only central Prague cinema for European arthouse movies, cult documentaries and mainstream and nonmainstream hits. Tucked away in yet another shopping arcade, it regularly shows Czech classics subtitled into English and participates in film festivals. The box office and film poster and DVD store (open 10am to 8pm) are opposite the bar and two screening rooms.

✪ LATERNA MAGIKA Theatre

☎ 224 931 482; www.laterna.cz; Nova Scéna theatre, Národní třída 4; tickets 680Kč; ⏱ box office 10am-8pm Mon-Sat; Ⓜ Národní Třída

A type of nonverbal performance combining dance, music, film and light, Laterna Magika is a much-touted part of the national heritage developed in the late 1950s. Frankly, though, the past is where its kitschy Black Light performances like Casanova and Legend of the Argonauts probably belong. They're best appreciated with an extremely camp sense of humour. The theatre is an interesting Socialist relic at least.

✪ LUCERNA MUSIC BAR Club

☎ 224 217 108; http://musicbar.iquest.cz; Lucerna pasáž, Štěpánská 61/Vodičkova 36; cover 100Kč; ⏱ 8pm-4am; Ⓜ Můstek or Ⓣ 3, 9, 14 or 24 to Václavské náměstí, night tram 55, 56, 58

Wey-hey! At a Friday or Saturday night's 1980s/'90s video party here, you might almost think you were in northern England, as weekending easyJet-setters who knew these tunes the first time around rub shoulders with fresh-faced Erasmus students, who didn't. It's a bit of mindless fun in an unpretentious school-disco-type atmosphere. On other nights, this old theatre hosts frequent live gigs.

⭐ MINOR THEATRE *Theatre*

Divadlo Minor; ☎ 222 231 351; www .minor.cz; Vodičkova 6; ☽ box office 10am-1.30pm & 2.30-8pm Mon-Fri, 11am-6pm Sat & Sun; Ⓜ Karlovo Náměstí; ♿

This children's theatre offers a fun mix of puppets, clown shows and pantomime. Performances (in Czech) are at 9.30am Monday to Friday and at 6pm or 7.30pm Tuesday to Thursday, and you can usually get a ticket at the door before the show.

⭐ NATIONAL THEATRE *Theatre*

Národní divadlo; ☎ info 224 901 448, tickets 224 901 377; www.narodni-divadlo.cz; Národní třída 2; tickets 30-750Kč; ☽ box office 10am-6pm; Ⓜ Národní Třída

Notable for its ornate golden roof, the National Theatre was erected in the late 19th century as part of the Czech National Revival of culture. Despite recent sackings and administrative upheavals, it's preserved its excellent reputation for drama, opera and ballet. English subtitles are provided for operas but not for plays. Many of the ballet performances are staged in the allied Estates Theatre (p93).

⭐ REDUTA JAZZ CLUB *Club*

☎ 224 933 487; www.redutajazzclub .cz; Národní třída 20; cover 300Kč;

Catch a gig at Prague's oldest jazz club, Reduta

🕒 box office from 3pm Mon-Fri, from 7pm Sat & Sun, venue 9pm-3am; Ⓜ Národní Třída, night tram 53, 57, 58, 59

Prague's oldest jazz club was founded in 1958 during the communist era, but is best known as the venue where US president Bill Clinton played the saxophone in 1994. It has an intimate setting, with smartly dressed (and sometimes bored-looking) patrons squeezing into tiered seats and lounges to soak up the big-band, swing and dixieland atmosphere. You can also book ahead through www.ticketpro.cz.

⭐ **STATE OPERA** *Theatre*

Státní opera Praha; ☎ 224 227 266; www.opera.cz; Wilsonova 4; opera tickets 50-1150Kč, ballet tickets 50-800Kč; 🕒 box office 10am-5.30pm Mon-Fri, 10am-noon & 1-5.30pm Sat & Sun; Ⓜ Muzeum

The State Opera's ballet troupe has been wooing international audiences on recent tours, and its opera ensemble has also had one or two recent hits, so it's always worth investigating their home performances in this impressive neo-rococo building. An annual Verdi festival takes place in August and September.

⭐ **VAGON** *Club*

☎ 221 085 599; www.vagon.cz; Národní třída 25; 🕒 6pm-5am Mon-Sat, to 1am Sun; Ⓜ Národní Třída, night tram 53, 57, 58, 59

Old Czech rockers never die; they just go to Vagon ('wagon'). But they're joined by plenty of youngsters in this long, narrow venue, where stencils of heroes like Mick Jagger watch from the walls while folk-punk groups, Red Hot Chilli Pepper cover bands or crusty old Velvet Revolution legends the Plastic People of the Universe (see p174) take the stage for the nightly gigs. Look for the passageway beside KFC.

> VINOHRADY & ŽIŽKOV

Uphill from the Old and New Towns, neighbouring Vinohrady and Žižkov are the odd couple that shouldn't get on, but do.

Bourgeois Vinohrady takes its name from having been Emperor Charles IV's vineyards, and it still boasts high-ceilinged, Art Nouveau apartment buildings from when it was developed in the late 19th century. After 1989 it became popular with arty foreign expats and was the first residential district to become gentrified. Its touchstones are náměstí Míru, restaurant-lined Manesova street, sloping Vinohradská and the hillside Riegrovy sady (park).

The 'people's republic' of Žižkov, by contrast, is historically working class, rebellious and revolutionary. Famous for its numerous pubs, cheap beer, alternative nightlife, TV tower and relative multiethnicity, it still proudly displays the flag (green, white and red) from its days as an independent Austro-Hungarian town. It was also the first suburb after 1989 to reintroduce the bohemian carnival of Masopust (p27). But what's this real estate agents are calling Žižkov recently? 'Lower Vinohrady'? Oh dear – better get there soon.

VINOHRADY & ŽIŽKOV

NEIGHBOURHOODS

VINOHRADY & ŽIŽKOV

SEE

CHURCH OF THE MOST SACRED HEART OF OUR LORD

Kostel Nejsvětějšího Srdce Páně; náměstí Jiřího z Poděbrad 19; M Jiřího z Poděbrad

In the green square above Jiřího z Poděbrad metro stands one of Europe's great modern churches. Square-angled and blocky, the unusual Sacred Heart (1932) merges classical Greek and cubist influences. Its façade is glazed brown-brick, while its massive, tombstone-like bell tower features an enormous see-through clock. The church is the work of Jože Plečník, the Slovenian architect who revamped Prague Castle in the early 20th century. In 2007 it was up for possible Unesco World Heritage listing.

JEWISH CEMETERY

Židovské hřbitovy; Izraelská 1; admission free; 9am-5pm Sun-Thu, to 2pm Fri Apr-Oct, 9am-4pm Sun-Thu, to 2pm Fri Nov-Mar, last entry 30min before closing, closed Jewish holidays; M Želivského

The grave of Franz Kafka (1883–1924) is the most visited in this leafy cemetery. The writer lies buried with his parents opposite a plaque for his friend Max Brod; turn right at row 21, then left at the wall until you come to the end of the sector. Fans commemorate Kafka's death on 3 June.

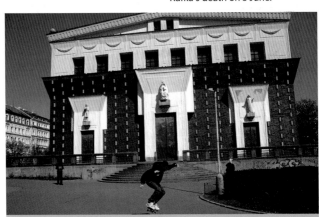

Skate by the modern Church of the Most Sacred Heart of Our Lord

Visit the hilltop Vítkov National Monument

◉ OLŠANY CEMETERY
Olšanské hřbitovy; Vinohradská 153; admission free; ☺ 8am-7pm May-Sep, 8am-6pm Mar, Apr & Oct, 9am-4pm Nov-Feb; Ⓜ Flora

Huge and atmospheric, Prague's main burial ground was founded in 1680, but is known for a relatively recent grave. Jan Palach, the student who set himself on fire in 1969 in protest at the Soviet invasion (see p100), is buried to the right of the main gate.

◉ VÍTKOV NATIONAL MONUMENT
Národní památník Vítkov; ☎ 222 781 676; www.pamatnik-vitkov.cz; U památníku 1900; Ⓜ Florenc

This hilltop monument (great views) commemorates 15th-century Hussite commander and independence fighter Jan Žižka, with a huge, 9m-tall equestrian statue of the one-eyed warrior after whom Žižkov is named. The embalmed body of communist president Klement Gottwald once rested in the accompanying mausoleum, until the corpse went a bit mouldy. Now the mausoleum is set to reopen as a history museum in 2009.

◉ ŽIŽKOV TOWER
Žižkovská věž; ☎ 267 005 778; www.tower.cz; Mahlerovy sady 1; adult/student/child 150/120/60Kč; ☺ 10am-11pm; Ⓜ Jiřího z Poděbrad

Hideous or futuristic? *Miminka*, the 10 giant babies crawling up Prague's TV transmitter, have quelled such debates about this structure (1985–1992), as people just enjoy the quirkiness that sculptor David Černý has brought to the city's tallest landmark. Attractively lighting the 216m needle at night helps, too. High-speed lifts go to a 93m observation deck, but many people prefer the view from Petřín Lookout Tower. The 66m restaurant

HOW THE TOWER GOT ITS BABIES

Žižkov Tower first acquired its clinging babies in 2000 as an art installation during Prague's reign as a European City of Culture. They came down at the end of that tenure, but the resulting public outcry meant they were reinstated, and should now be there until 2010 at least.

Meanwhile, creator David Černý (see p23) has continued to court controversy. In 2006 his sculpture of Saddam Hussein in a giant fish tank (a satire of BritArtist Damien Hirst's shark, *The Physical Impossibility of Death in the Mind of Someone Living*) was temporarily banned in Belgium and Poland. He's now developing an arts centre, called Meet.

is dreadful and overpriced, and a film on the windows affects the admittedly expansive panorama (up to 100km on a good day).

SHOP

SHAKESPEARE & SONS *Books*
☎ 271 740 839; www.shakes.cz; Krymská 12; 🕑 10am-7pm; 🚊 4, 22, 23
Though it stocks plenty of English novels, 'Shakes' is more than a bookshop – it's a congenial literary hangout, with a café (open till midnight) that regularly hosts poetry readings, author events and live jazz, and where you can settle down for a read over coffee and cakes.

Giant babies crawl up the side of the Žižkov Tower

⊞ EAT

⊞ AMBIENTE
International $$-$$$

☎ 222 727 851; www.ambi.cz; Mánesova 59; ⊙ 11am-midnight Mon-Fri, noon-midnight Sat & Sun; Ⓜ Jiřího z Poděbrad
The first in a chain of bizarrely titled 'living restaurants', this cheerful, truly atmospheric Vinohrady restaurant still buzzes. The American barbecue ribs, fajitas, steaks and chicken wings are complemented by tasty pasta dishes, salads and some excellent house wines.

⊞ AROMI *Italian* $$$-$$$$
☎ 222 713 222; Mánesova 78; ⊙ noon-11pm Mon-Sat, noon-10pm Sun; Ⓜ Jiřího z Poděbrad
This gourmet Italian restaurant, specialising in cuisine from the Marché region, enjoys an exulted reputation and certainly the rustic setting is appealing. With chunky, polished wooden tables set well apart and a central display of imported delicacies, the place is businesslike at lunch and romantic in the evenings. Choose between the renowned seafood or rarities like *Vincisgrassi alla Marchigiana* (a rich lasagne). Unfortunately, one barely edible *Gnocchi mare e monti* (gnocchi with clams and chanterelles) has taught us that Aromi isn't above all the usual Prague problems with inconsistency.

⊞ LA LAVANDE
French $$$-$$$$

☎ 222 517 406; www.lalavande.cz; Záhřebská 24; ⊙ 11.30am-3pm & 6.30-11pm Mon-Fri, 6.30-11pm Sat; Ⓜ Náměstí Míru
Top-quality gourmet cuisine and a chintzy French farmhouse interior make this perfect for a special occasion. Choose between a room decorated with Persian rugs, upholstered chairs and mirrors, or the relaxing garden, to sample such delights as foie gras served with fig sauce, baked banana and strawberries or lamb stuffed with prosciutto, spinach, potatoes and parmesan.

⊞ MOZAIKA *International* $$$
☎ 224 253 011; www.restaurant mozaika.cz; Nitranská 13; ⊙ 11.30am-midnight Mon-Fri, 2pm-midnight Sat, 4pm-midnight Sun; Ⓜ Jirvího z Poděbrad
Popular with expats and business travellers, Mozaika is slick but not particularly atmospheric. Yet it's one of Prague's true shining lights because of its almost always excellent food. The contemporary bistro-style menu includes the likes of sushi, lamb confit, Thai mussels and a famous burger. Even the unlikely sounding butter-fish (with onion mash, tapenade and tomato salsa) proves delicious. Rich desserts are best shared.

🍴 RADOST FX Vegetarian $$

☎ 224 254 776; www.radostfx.cz; Bělehradská 120; ⏱ 11.30am-2am; Ⓜ IP Pavlova, night tram 51, 56, 57, 59

This veteran veggie has been around too long to ignore, and its American-style weekend brunches are still a highlight (if you're patient). Joined by a video store and club (p128), the restaurant comprises a funky, vaguely Gothic café and a newer, more harem-like lounge. Smoothies are delicious; food is variable. Be prepared for the extra service charge on the bill.

🍴 TIGER TIGER Thai $-$$

☎ 222 512 048; Anny Letenské 5; ⏱ 11.30am-11pm Mon-Fri, 5-11pm Sat & Sun; Ⓜ Náměstí Míru; ✗ Ⓥ

Tiger Tiger's tiny front yellow-and-blue dining room expands out the back into two further areas, one nonsmoking. Although the restaurant serves some of the city's best Thai cuisine, meat and seafood dishes tend to be tastier than vegetarian – handy to remember when choosing weekday lunch deals (11.30am to 3pm; 100Kč to 140Kč for soup and a main).

🍸 DRINK

BLIND EYE Bar

www.blindeye.cz; Vlkova 26; ⏱ 7pm-5am; 🚋 5, 9, 26 to Husinecká, night tram 55, 58

The owners keep the lighting very low in this scurrilous little speakeasy-style bar, because they reckon we all look better that way. Here a mix of expats and Žižkov locals lounge around, play table football or quaff the legendary 'Adios m*therf*cker' cocktails. Thursday's electroclash DJ evenings sees the place particularly mobbed.

🍸 HAPU Bar

☎ 222 720 158; Orlická 8; ⏱ 6pm-2am; Ⓜ Jiřího z Poděbrad, night tram 51, 57, 59

Visiting Hapu is like popping around for a drink in a popular friend's living room. This shabby-chic, shallow basement is jam-packed even on weeknights, with a familiar, frequently English-speaking crew who feel comfortable enough to bring the dog along if they please. The whole point, though, is that the place mixes a mean cocktail – arguably the best in town – with freshly squeezed fruit juices.

🍸 KAVÁRNA KAABA Café

☎ 222 254 021; www.kaaba.cz; Mánesova 20; ⏱ 8am-10pm Mon-Fri, 9am-10pm Sat, 10am-10pm Sun; 🚋 11 to Italská; ♿

Stylish Kaaba flaunts retro furniture and pastel-coloured décor that could have come straight from the award-winning Czech pavilion at the 1958 Brussels Expo proud (see the boxed text, right). Gourmet imported coffee (including Jamaican Blue Mountain), snacks and an extensive list of Czech and imported wines are served, while the in-house *trafik* (news and tobacco counter) is neatly ordered to the nearest millimetre.

KUŘE V HODINKÁCH Pub

☎ 222 734 212; Seifertova 26;
🕑 11am-1am Mon-Fri, noon-1am Sat, 6pm-1am Sun; 🚊 5, 9, 26 to Lipanská or Husinecká, night tram 55, 58

'The Chicken in the Watch' is relatively posh for Žižkov, attracting slightly better-heeled locals, particularly to its downstairs music bar. With a name harking back to a 1970s Czech album, it's kitted out with eye-catching rock paraphernalia, but its choice of different beer brands (an unusual occurrence in Prague), malt whiskies (including some connoisseurs' favourites like Lagavulin) and unexpectedly tasty food are the real reasons for visiting.

POPOCAFÉPETL Café/Bar

☎ 777 944 672; www.popocafepetl.cz; Italská 18; 🕑 10am-1am Mon-Fri, 4pm-1am Sat & Sun; Ⓜ Náměstí Míru, night tram 51, 57, 59

Before 6pm this is like a moody version of a teenage American milk-bar but thankfully pulls in a crowd of 20-somethings in the eve-

---

NOT BIG IN BELGIUM

Design buffs beware. When Czechs talk of the Brussels style, they're not referring to Belgian Art Nouveau or anything related to Henry Van de Velde. Rather, they're harking back to a heyday of their own national design, when despite the constraints of working under a communist regime Czechoslovakia triumphed with its circular restaurant pavilion at the 1958 Brussels Expo. More than 100 local designers took away awards, including porcelain designer Jaroslav Ježek, who won the Grand Prix for his Elka coffee service.

The aesthetics of the time were similar to Kaaba's, opposite. For a more authentic take, visit Veletržní Palace (p133).

---

nings. By the time you read this, the branch in Malá Strana (p69) might have become more popular, or closed – popular PopoCafé always seems to be moving.

RIEGROVY SADY PARK CAFÉ
Beer Garden

Riegrovy sady; 🕑 depending on weather, at least Apr-Oct; Ⓜ Náměstí Míru or 🚊 11 to Italsk

On a balmy evening, you often hear this huge, German-style beer garden atop Riegrovy sady before you see it; a noise like waves breaking, interspersed with the heavy chink of sturdy glasses, rumbles out from under the trees. Inside, hundreds of Vinohrady and Žižkov denizens (and their dogs) are making merry with cheap Gambrinus, poured at a super-speedy rate to keep the perpetual queue moving.

� SAHARA CAFÉ *Café*
☎ 222 514 987; www.saharacafe.com; náměstí Míru 6/Ibsenova 1; ⏰ 8am-midnight Mon-Sat, 11am-11pm Sun; Ⓜ Náměstí Míru

This designer souk looks fantastic, with a merger of neutral stone, rattan chairs, teak and mahogany tables, Moroccan pillows, embroidered drapes and palm fronds throughout its unfolding warren of rooms. (Don't forget to explore the downstairs garden in summer.) Sadly, the Mediterranean and North African food doesn't live up to the interiors, so stick to drinks.

Quench your thirst at the Sahara Café

� SAINTS *Bar*
☎ 222 250 326; www.praguesaints.cz; Polská 32; ⏰ 5pm-4am; Ⓜ Náměstí Míru, night tram 51, 57, 59

Sealing the deal on Prague's booming 'gay quarter' in Vinohrady (see p161), this British-run bar is laidback, friendly and serves decent drinks. With a multinational staff speaking many languages, for newcomers it's the perfect entrée to the local scene.

� U SADU *Pub*
☎ 222 727 072; www.usadu.cz; Škroupovo náměstí; ⏰ 8am-4am Mon-Fri, 9am-4am Sat & Sun; Ⓜ Jiřího z Poděbrad, night tram 51, 57, 59

Another great neighbourhood pub popular with old locals, expat students and gruff staff, this has a smoky ground-floor room bedecked with communist-era public notices, helmets, gas masks and other bizarre knick-knacks.

� U VYSTŘELENÉHO OKA *Pub*
☎ 226 278 714; U Božích bojovníků 3; ⏰ 4.30pm-1am Mon-Sat; 🚌 133, 207 to U Památníku

You have to love a pub with vinyl pads on the wall above the gents' urinals for weary drinkers. 'The Shot-Out Eye' – the name refers to the one-eyed Hussite hero commemorated on the hill behind the pub (see p121) – is a typically

PUB CRAWL ALONG BOŘIVOJOVA

With allegedly 300-plus pubs over 650 hectares, Žižkov claims to have more pubs per square metre than anywhere else in the world. The biggest density of these is found along the legendary Bořivojova street. If you walk the four blocks between the tram stop at Lipanská and Riegrovy sady in Vinohrady and count all the drinking dens of various descriptions you can see along or from the street, you'll tally just under 30. Locals declare no-one's ever conquered the street by having a drink in each; in fact, it's not even sensible to try. However, this is a good if grungy little strip for keeping your options open. Start at **U Houdků** (☎ 222 711 239; Bořivojova 110; ☺ 10am-11pm), a place with a beer garden, much beloved of backpackers and students.

grungy and raucous Žižkov hostelry and beer garden.

 **WINGS CLUB** *Bar*
☎ 222 713 151; www.wingsclub.cz; Lucemburská 11; ☺ 11.30am-11pm; Ⓜ Jiřího z Poděbrad
Shaped like a small aeroplane hangar, this theme bar is lined with Czech aeronautical memorabilia from WWII, with photographs and uniforms and even an entire propeller mounted on one wall.

 PLAY

⭐ **INFINITY** *Club*
☎ 272 176 580; www.infinitybar.cz; Chrudimská 2a/2526; ☺ 10pm-3am Mon-Sat; Ⓜ Flora, night tram 51
Smart-casual clubbing gear is the order of the day in this midsized cellar, where the clientele seems a tad sleeker than usual. Alternating between upbeat happy house and nostalgic '60s to '90s nights, it's much more enjoyable than its

reputation as the second-biggest pick-up joint in Prague might suggest. (We're not telling you the first!) Follow the crowds from nearby Flora metro station and down through the middle of the ground-floor restaurant.

⭐ **LE CLAN** *Club*
☎ 272 176 580; www.leclan.cz; Balbínova 23; ☺ from 10pm Tue-Sat; 🚊 11 to Italská, night tram 51, 57, 59
Not really happening until 3am and often running to the next day's noon, this is Prague's leading after-party venue. Buzz yourself in and take a seat in the sofa-bedecked basement or join the bods dancing. Want to see what the place runs on? Just pop into the toilets and check out the strategically mounted horizontal mirrors.

⭐ **PALÁC AKROPOLIS** *Club*
☎ 296 330 911; www.palacakropolis.cz; Kubelíkova 27; cover free-30Kč; ☺ club 7pm-5am; 🚊 5, 9, 26, night tram 51, 57, 59

This huge Prague institution is a sticky-floored shrine to alternative music and drama with a broad cross section of regulars. Its trump card is its innovative roster of gigs, from Boban Markovic to Sigur Ros to the Strokes. Otherwise, when the 850-capacity concert hall is shut and all you have is the speakeasy vibe in the two smaller DJ bars, the place's appeal might be a bit difficult for newcomers to fathom.

⭐ RADOST FX Club

☎ 224 254 776; www.radostfx.cz; Bělehradská 120; cover 100-300Kč; 🕙 10pm-6am; Ⓜ IP Pavlova, night tram 51, 56, 57, 59

Another Prague stalwart, Radost is a high-profile, fairly mainstream club that pulls in big-name DJs and shiny punters. There's a chilled-out, bohemian atmosphere, with Moroccan-boudoir-meets-Moulin-Rouge décor and the upstairs lounge serves food late. Thursday's hip-hop night, FXbounce (www.fxbounce.com), is a weekly highlight.

⭐ SEDM VLKŮ Club

☎ 222 711 725; www.sedmvlku.cz; Vlkova 7; 🕙 5pm-3am Mon-Sat; 🚊 5, 9, 26

'Seven Wolves' is a cool, two-level, art-studenty café-bar and club – at street level there's candlelight, friendly staff, weird wrought-iron

work and funky murals; down in the darkened cellar DJs pump out techno, breakbeat, drum'n'bass and ragga from 9pm on Friday and Saturday nights.

⭐ TERMIX Club

☎ 222 710 462; www.club-termix.cz; Třebízského 4a; admission free; 🕙 8pm-5am Wed-Sun; Ⓜ Náměstí Míru or Jiřího z Poděbrad, night tram 51, 57, 59

Although losing its number-one slot to the newer Valentino, Termix is still popular on the gay scene. There's an industrial-looking bar (with a car sticking out of one wall), smallish dance floor and dark room. The leading Wednesday night goes native with Czech pop tunes and is nicknamed 'Hezky Cesky' after the cute Czech customers.

⭐ VALENTINO Club

☎ 222 513 491; www.club-valentino.cz; Vinohradská 40; admission free; 🕙 from 11am; Ⓜ Náměstí Míru, night tram 51, 57, 59

Prague's one true gay super-club, Valentino boasts three floors, two dance floors, four bars and two dark rooms; and it's particularly packed and sweaty on the weekends. The music alternates between cool house and cheesy Czech pop, depending where exactly in the complex you drift.

Nush Imogen
Artist, musician and long-term Žižkov resident

London has Camden, New York has Greenwich Village and Prague has Žižkov. What's so cool about this district? It's more multicultural and less 'stiff' than the centre – yet only a short ride away. People here are more open and friendly, plus there are great music clubs, traditional pubs, seedy, nonstop gambling places *(Hernas)*, cafés, pizzerias, Czech bars, American bars, gay bars, etc. **It does have a reputation for pubs, doesn't it?** Yes. My street only has two blocks, but 11 places where you can get a drink. **Top spots?** Blind Eye (p124) is my late-evening favourite. Sedm Vlků (opposite) just for a beer with friends (good beer, by the way). And the Riegrovy sady beer garden (p125). **Do the sightseeing attractions interest you?** The TV Tower (p121) looks fantastic. We used to call that 'Prague's penis' when I was a kid. My friends once went to a fashion show and DJ party in the National Monument's mausoleum (p121) and loved it. **Any neighbourhood downsides?** Plenty of dog shit. Watch your step!

> HOLEŠOVICE

In Holešovice, you start to appreciate Prague as a genuine, working city rather than just a beautiful architectural theme park that attracts millions of visitors each year.

Sections of this former industrial quarter remain rundown, especially after 2002's devastating 'flood of the century'; but there are plans for a major dockside development and elsewhere the district is already gentrifying. New warehouse apartments are going up by the river and several leading clubs have moved into abandoned flats, shops and factories.

Home to one of Prague's two main international train stations, Holešovice is also blessed with large open spaces. The huge garden of Letná is its most accessible stretch of green, spectacularly overlooking Staré Město – with a distinctive metronome and one of the city's best beer gardens, too. However, the district also houses the funfair-style delights of Výstaviště, the huge park of Stromovka and Prague's top two ice-hockey teams.

Before all this, however, don't forget to visit the modern art collection of Veletržní Palace, one of the city's truly impressive galleries.

HOLEŠOVICE

◉ SEE
Křižíkova Fountain	1	C1
Lapidarium	2	D2
Letná Gardens	3	B4
National Technical Museum	4	C3
Stromovka Park	5	C2
Veletržní Palace	6	D3
Výstaviště	7	D2

🍴 EAT
Fraktal	8	B3

🍸 DRINK
Le Tram	9	C3
Letná Beer Garden	10	C4

⭐ PLAY
Cross Club	11	E1
Face-to-Face	12	E4
HC Sparta Praha	13	D1
Mecca	14	F2
Misch Masch	15	C3
Wakata	16	C2

SEE

LETNÁ GARDENS & TERRACE

Letenské sady; 🚊 **12, 17 to Čechův most**
There are great views from this vast park, but the socialist overtones of its huge concrete terrace are almost as interesting. In the 1950s the world's largest statue of Stalin was built here, only to be blown up in 1962. Today, the space is occupied by skateboarders, a beer garden (see p135) and artist Vratislav Karel Novák's huge **metronome**, symbolising the passage of time.

NATIONAL TECHNICAL MUSEUM

Národní technické muzeum; ☎ **220 399 111; www.ntm.cz; Kostelní 42; adult/ child 70/30Kč;** ⏱ **9am-5pm Tue-Fri, 10am-6pm Sat & Sun;** 🚊 **1, 8,15, 25, 26 to Letenské náměstí**
Always a highly rated attraction for its collection of vintage trains, planes and automobiles, including imperial Austro-Hungarian rail carriages, old Škoda and Tatra cars and Jawa motorcycles, this museum is due to reopen in July 2008 after major refurbishment. Check online for the latest.

Take in the views from the terrace at Letná Gardens

OH, HOW WE LAUGHED AT ŠKODA…

During the communist era, Czechoslovakia's less-than-perfect Škoda car became the butt of much the same jokes as East Germany's Trabant – although the Škoda was more ridiculed abroad than at home. Indeed, when Volkswagen bought the firm in 1991, its UK ads used the self-deprecating 'It's a Škoda, honest' to sell its seriously improved models. Jokes still linger about the older Škodas (the name means damage) in the National Technical Museum. But Škoda is now one of Europe's most successful brands, so it looks like it is having the last laugh.

> What do you call a Škoda with twin exhaust pipes? A wheelbarrow.

> How do you double the value of a Škoda? Fill the petrol tank.

> A guy walks into a garage and asks 'Can you give me a petrol cap for my Škoda?' The mechanic thinks about it briefly and replies, 'OK, sounds like a fair swap.'

> What's the difference between a door-to-door salesman and a Škoda? You can shut the door on a door-to-door salesman.

> Have you seen the ads asking 'What's behind the new Škoda?' The answer's not really 'Volkswagen', it's 'people pushing it'.

🄶 STROMOVKA PARK
🚊 5, 12, 14, 15, 17 to Výstaviště
Prague's largest central park was a medieval hunting ground for royals, now it's popular with strollers, joggers, cyclists and inline skaters. A new Mucha exhibition (see p100) might be built here in coming years.

🄶 VELETRŽNÍ PALACE
☎ 224 301 122, 222 321 459; www.ng prague.cz; Dukelských hrdinů 47; adult/concession any 1 floor from 100/50Kč, all 4 floors 250/120Kč, 3-8pm 1st Wed of month free; 🕙 10am-6pm Tue-Sun; 🚊 12, 14, 17 to Veletržní; 🕭
It takes an hour just to jog through this enormous functionalist building, housing the National Gallery's jaw-droppingly impressive collection of 19th-, 20th- and 21st-century Czech and European art. However, if you catch the vertiginous all-glass lift from the Small Hall to the 5th floor you'll get a quick overview of the atrium displays. Otherwise, make sure to circle the 3rd floor for Czech cubist masterpieces and French impressionist works, before popping into the 1958 Expo exhibit on the 2nd.

🄶 VÝSTAVIŠTĚ
☎ 220 103 111; Tue-Fri free, Sat & Sun 20Kč; 🕙 2-9pm Tue-Fri, 10am-9pm Sat & Sun; 🅼 Nádraží Holešovice or 🚊 5, 12, 14, 15, 17 to Výstaviště
If your short break to Prague is becoming longer, visit the ornate wrought-iron Výstaviště building, erected for the 1891 Jubilee

Exhibition. Behind it is the kitsch dancing **Křižíkova Fountain** (☎ 220 103 280; www.krizikovafontana.cz; shows around 200Kč; ☺ performances hourly 8-11pm Mar-Oct), which performs to music. In the nearby **Lapidarium** (☎ 233 375 636; adult/child 20/10Kč; ☺ noon-6pm Tue-Fri, 10am-6pm Sat & Sun) stand 10 of Charles Bridge's original statues, among others. Between February and Easter the park becomes a funfair (see p27).

🍴 EAT

🍴 FRAKTAL
Mexican/International $

☎ 777 794 094; www.fraktalbar.cz; Šmeralová 1; ☺ 11am-1am, food 11am-11pm; 🚋 1,8,15, 25, 26 to Letenské náměstí, night tram 51, 56; Ⓥ

This low-lit cellar feels like a genuine neighbourhood eatery and watering hole, with Czech and expat regulars treating the staff like old friends. Newcomers are made to feel welcome, too. Although the nightly focus is on beer (Pilsner Urquell, Gambrinus and Kozel), the food is well-produced. Mexican dishes, steaks, salads and gourmet burgers are crowned by excellent weekend brunches (till 3.30pm).

🍸 DRINK

🍸 LE TRAM *Bar*

☎ 233 370 359; Šmeralová 12; ☺ 8pm-6am; 🚋 1,8,15, 25, 26 to Letenské náměstí, night tram 51, 56
Looking like it's been furnished from a Prague public-transport

Relax over a cold Gambinus at the Letná Beer Garden

AN OCTOPUS FOR LETNÁ?

In a historic city like Prague, modern architecture is always controversial, and some of the best Czech architects today practise abroad. Jan Kaplický is a perfect example. His company, Future Systems, has won worldwide acclaim for its space-age media centre at Lord's Cricket Ground in London and the Selfridges store in Birmingham, England, but he's never built a thing in Prague.

Now Kaplický has won the competition to build the new National Library in Letná Gardens before 2011 and it's causing debate. His design – actually like a golden sheet thrown over a cube – has been compared to a colourful octopus. The director of the National Gallery, Milan Knížák, has publicly claimed this might be too bold for Letná (erm, the park that once housed the world's largest statue of Stalin?). Others have welcomed Kaplický's innovation.

closing-down sale, this pleasantly scruffy French-owned bar is filled with plastic seats and benches salvaged from decommissioned trams, plus other 1970s *objets trouvés*. It pulls in a truly international crowd with cheap beer, lively conversation and cool tunes.

LETNÁ BEER GARDEN
Beer Garden

Letná Gardens; 11am-11.30pm; 12, 17 to Čechův most

Spread along a shaded but dusty escarpment at the eastern end of Letná Gardens, this slew of rickety benches provides one of the city's best views, looking across the river to the spires of Stare Město, and southwest to Malá Strana. You can rely on its being open June to September, but you'll often find it

serving up Gambrinus on sunny winter days, too.

PIVOVAR U BULOVKY *Pub*
☎ 284 800 650; Bulovka 17; 11am-11pm Mon-Thu, 11am-midnight Fri, noon-midnight Sat; 10, 15, 24, 25 to Bulovka

This initially unassuming suburban pub and microbrewery soon reveals why it's such a city legend. It's not just the range of award-winning beers, although these include a delicious house *ležak* (lager) as well as ales, stouts, Düsseldorf-style *Alts* and Bavarian-like *Weissbiers*. Part of the pub's appeal is its welcoming hum and local atmosphere. Staff don't always speak English, but it's not hard to make yourself understood.

František Richter
Award-winning brewer & owner of Pivovar U Bulovky (p135)

I'm visiting Prague and want to sample some beer. Where should I start
Out of the city centre. It's full of tourists and the prices are bloody high, so it
better to go to the inner suburbs like Vinohrady, Žižkov or Karlín. **What sort
of beer are best?** Actually, Czechs don't have as many types of beer as the
Belgians, British or Irish. We drink 99.9% lager. **Any hints here?** Most drinke
prefer Czech *světlé* (light) beers. Industrial beer – from the big brands –
tastes insipid to me. Beer from microbreweries [see, for example, the Best
Microbreweries list, p153] is often fresher and cleaner tasting. **Indeed,
you're one of those microbreweries and you've twice won 'brewer of
the year'.** Yes, there are some 'exotics' like me who specialise in the old bee
types – Czech beer like you used to get 100 years ago. **Good atmosphere
too?** There are days when all the guests are dancing on the table. (Laughs.)

PLAY

ABATON Club

☎ 296 330 980; http://abaton.fanonline
.cz; Na Košince 8, off Povltavská 2175;
admission 200-400Kč; 🚋 10, 15, 24, 25 to
Stejskalova

This enormous, atmospheric ware-house complex hosts everything from Prodigy concerts and dance-music awards to the annual Sperm electronic music festival (see p27) and benefit gigs for Tibet. Although it's out in the industrial wastelands, it's worth the trip for its array of different scenes – chic cocktail bars, down-and-dirty table football and more – throughout its warren of bars and rooms.

CROSS CLUB Club

☎ 296 330 980; www.crossclub
.cz; Plynární 23; admission 50-100Kč;
🕓 4pm-late; Ⓜ Nádraží Holešovice,
night tram 53, 54

An eclectic programme from D&B, jungle, dub and reggae to electro, techno and live music goes on in this bar, but the main attraction is the venue itself. Both the ground floor and basement of a rundown apartment block have been trans-formed into a work of industrial or sci-fi art, with glowing homemade lighting installations, kinetic sculptures formed from bits of junk metal, film reels, engine parts

and even a bus outside. Alterna-tive and unique.

FACE-TO-FACE Club

☎ 242 498 353; www.facetoface.cz;
Ostrov Štvanice 1125; cover 100Kč, all-inclusive parties 250-350Kč; 🕓 9pm-6am
Wed, Fri & Sat; Ⓜ Florenc, night tram 56

Cheap drinks, plus 'all-inclusive' parties where your entry fee cov-ers wine, beer and soft drinks, pull in a very young mix of locals and foreigners on a budget. Otherwise, mainstream dance music, DJs and emcees fuel the uncomplicated party atmosphere in this former exhibition hall.

HC SLAVIA PRAHA Sport

☎ 266 121 111; www.hc-slavia.cz; Sazka
Arena, Ocelářská 2; tickets 140-590Kč;
🕓 box office 1-5pm on day of game;
Ⓜ Českomoravská

Although Sparta is the leading Czech team, Slavia has been clos-ing on it fast in recent years. It al-ready has one advantage with this 18,000-capacity stadium, built to host the Ice Hockey World Cham-pionship in April 2004. Tickets can be booked online at www
.saskaarena.com.

HC SPARTA PRAHA Sport

☎ 266 727 443; www.hcsparta.cz,
www.ticketpro.cz; T-Mobile Arena,
Za elektrárnou 419; tickets 60-220Kč;
🕓 box office 7.30-11am & noon-4pm

NEIGHBOURHOODS
HOLEŠOVICE

Mon-Fri, weekends according to season;
Ⓜ Nádraží Holešovice or 🚊 5, 12, 14, 15, 17 to Výstaviště

The Czechs are *meisters* of ice-hockey, with the national team long rated among the world's best; and although many Czech stars now ply their trade in the US, Prague teams Sparta and Slavia still display a level of skill that's astounding for the price of their tickets. Sparta's arena has seen better days and the small crowds rattle around it early in the season, but it's the leading team and things come to life in the February to early March play-offs. Online tickets are available at www.ticketpro.cz.

☆ MECCA Club

☎ 283 870 522; www.mecca.cz; U průhonu 3; cover Fri & Sat 90-690Kč, Wed & Thu free; 🕐 10pm-6am Wed-Sat; 🚊 5, 12, 15 to U Průhonu, night tram 54

A slice of Ibiza in the Prague suburbs, Mecca is a premier name on the city's clubbing scene. Its black-walled interior is sultry and sexy, with the relatively small, DJ-dominated dance floor reached via a restaurant area popular with models, film stars and fashionistas, while there's a chill-out lounge with curvy couches downstairs. On weekends some more pretentious punters fumble around in sunglasses. The midweek '80s/'90s night is more relaxed.

☆ MISCH MASCH Club

☎ 603 272 227; www.mischmasch.cz; Veletržní 61; cover 100Kč, women before 10pm 50Kč; 🕐 8pm-6am Wed-Sat; 🚊 1, 8,15, 25, 26 to Letenské náměstí, night tram 51, 56

Good-time house and hip-hop is found at sticky-floored Misch Masch. Turn left for the large house area, with both female and (shock!) male podium dancers. To the right is the slightly more intimate hip-hop floor, bar and gallery. Fashionable without any unnecessary attitude, the place is popular with up-fer-it young locals, overseas students and a few older weekend-breakers. Watch for special themed evenings, too.

☆ WAKATA Club

☎ 233 370 518; www.wakata.cz; Malířská 14; admission free; 🕐 5pm-3am Mon-Thu, to 5am Fri & Sat, 6pm-3am Sun; 🚊 1, 8, 15, 25, 26 to Letenské náměstí, night tram 51, 56

There's no designer chic or style statements in this small, laid-back DJ lounge, full of colourful urban wall murals and some interestingly welded barstools. Enjoy inexpensive beers and cocktails as you bop along to a nightly soundtrack of funk, latin, dub, ambient, jungle, reggae or hip hop.

>WALKING TOURS

Charles Bridge

WALKING TOURS

MALÁ STRANA GARDENS

The aristocrats who inhabited 18th-century Malá Strana created beautiful gardens, many of which are now open to the public. Taking in two gardens and one park, this quick walk is best undertaken between April and October, when everything is in bloom.

Exiting Malostranská metro station, turn left at the top of the escalators and right just out of the building, into the little 'rabbit hole' door that leads to the **Wallenstein Garden** (1; p18), an oasis of relaxation in this busy district. Spend at least 15 minutes soaking up the special atmosphere, before departing the same way you came.

From Malostranská station, turn right onto Klárov, and go straight across the junction with the tram line, continuing along U lužického

Take in the views across the Vltava River from Kampa Island (p56)

semináře. Keep a sharp eye out for a gate on the right that leads to the **Vojan Gardens** (**2**). While less manicured that most Malá Strana's parks, this is a popular spot with locals, who like to come here to take a breather with the kids, sit in the sun on the park benches or even hold summer parties.

From the park continue to Hergetova Cihelná, where you can enjoy the David Černý sculpture **Piss** (**3**; p62) in front of the **Franz Kafka Museum** (**4**; p57). Have a little mischievous fun sending SMS messages to the sculptures, to change the way they pee.

Continue along U lužického semináře, and when the street narrows bear left across the little bridge over the Čertovka (Devil's Stream) onto **Kampa Island** (**5**; p57). Pass under Charles Bridge and emerge into the picturesque little square of Na Kampě. To the left, note the **metal plaques** (**6**) marking the level of the terrible 1890 and 2002 floods in Prague.

Head on through the square and into the leafy riverside park known simply as **Kampa** (**7**; from the Latin campus or 'field'), one of the city's favourite chill-out zones, usually littered with lounging bodies in summer.

If the mood strikes, go for a wander through the modern art collections of the **Kampa Museum** (**8**; p57) housed in a restored mill complex on the edge of the river.

distance 1.5km **duration** 40 minutes (including stop in Wallenstein Garden)
▶ **start** Ⓜ Malostranská ● **end**
🚊 Újezd

KAFKA'S PRAGUE

'This narrow circle encompasses my entire life,' Franz Kafka (1883–1924) once said, drawing an outline around Prague's Old Town. While an exaggeration – he travelled and died abroad – Prague is a constant, unspoken presence in Kafka's writing, and this walk through the Old Town passes some of his regular haunts.

The author's fiction was also influenced by his job as an insurance clerk in an earlier, sometimes brutal, industrial era. Kafka was employed for 14 years (1908–1922) at the **Worker's Accident Insurance Co** (**1**; Na poříčí 7), studying workplace accidents and recommending safety measures.

Heading home daily, he'd pass the **Powder Gate** (**2**; p77) and **Municipal House** (**3**; p75), which was then new. Stop for tea in the building's ornate café if you wish, before continuing along Celetná. Just before the Old Town Sq is the **House of the Three Kings** (**4**; Celetná 3), where the Kafkas lived

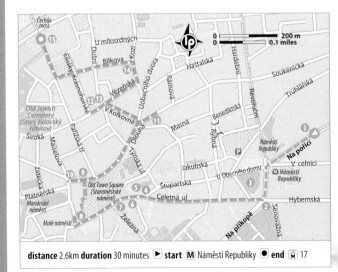

distance 2.6km **duration** 30 minutes ▶ **start** Ⓜ Náměstí Republiky ● **end** 🚊 17

from1896 to 1907. Here Franz first had his own room, overlooking the **Church of Our Lady Before Týn** (**5**; p74), and wrote his first story. Across Celetná, the **Sixt House** (**6**; Celetná 2) was an earlier childhood home (1888–89), and just metres away is **At the Unicorn** (**7**; Staroměstské náměstí 17), the home of Berta Fanta's regular literary salon. Kafka attended often with Max Brod, the friend who later published his writings (see p172).

The **House of the Minute** (**8**), the Renaissance corner building attached to the Old Town Hall, was where Franz lived as a young boy (1889–96), be-ing reluctantly dragged – he later recalled – to his school in Masná street by the family cook.

Just west of **Church of St Nicholas** (**9**) is **Kafka's birthplace** (**10**; p75), marked by a bust of the author at náměstí Franze Kafky 3 (formerly U Radnice 5). Stop to take a picture.

Despite several fraught love affairs, Kafka never married and mostly lived with his parents. But one of his few bachelor flats is found at **Dlouhá 16** (**11**). Continuing north past the **Franz Kafka monument** (**12**; p74) and the **Spanish Synagogue** (**13**; p79) you'll come to another at **Bilková 22** (**14**). In 1914 he began *The Trial* here.

Finally, head west to Pařížská and north towards the river. In the **Hotel Intercontinental's grounds** (**15**) stood another Kafka family apartment (1907–13). Between suicidally gazing at the water from his 3rd-floor win-dow, Franz wrote his Oedipal short story *The Judgment* (1912) and began *Metamorphosis,* about a man transformed into a giant insect.

Ceiling fresco of the Church of St Nicholas

VELVET REVOLUTION

It's nearly two decades since 1989's Velvet Revolution – when Czechs peacefully overthrew their communist masters – but it will always be a landmark event.

This walk starts where the revolution itself began, where Národní třída meets Mikulandská. Today, there's a **bronze sculpture (1)** under the arches here, marking the Masakr (massacre) of 17 November 1989 – when 50,000 students on an official march to remember Czechs murdered during WWII were attacked by riot police.

Head up Národní třída to Wenceslas Sq. En route, note beautiful **Adria Palace (2)**; it's important later.

The Masakr in Národní třída outraged the nation, and hundreds of thousands of protestors flooded into Wenceslas Sq the next night, staying for weeks. Approach the **Wenceslas Statue (3**; p105), which itself became a 'revolutionary', bedecked with flags, posters and political slogans. The nearby **Memorial to the Victims of Communism (4)** was the protestors' ad-hoc

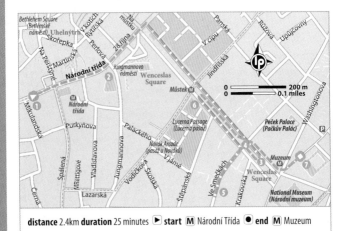

distance 2.4km **duration** 25 minutes ▶ **start** Ⓜ Národní Třída ● **end** Ⓜ Muzeum

monument to earlier martyr Jan Palach, who set himself on fire to protest against the Soviet crackdown on 1968's liberal 'Prague Spring'.

Meanwhile, Prague theatres swapped drama for public discussions. Head to **Činoherní Klub Theatre** (**5**; Ve Smečkách 26), where Civic Forum, the key dissident group led by playwright Václav Havel, formed on 19 November. It immediately demanded communist resignations and an investigation into the Masakr.

Remember Adria Palace? Civic Forum set up office there, holding daily press conferences and threatening a general strike.

Return to the **Melantrich building** (**6**; Wenceslas Sq 36), now a Marks & Spencer store. The revolution would continue for another month, but a milestone occurred here on 24 November. That evening, as 400,000 demonstrators waited for Havel to address them from the balcony, the deposed 'Prague Spring' president Alexander Dubček emerged first instead. He was reappearing in public after 20 years of enforced obscurity – even his name was banned – and he greeted the crowd: 'Czechoslovensko!' ('Czecho-slovakia!'). The crowd, BBC correspondent Allan Little recalls, 'roared in incredulity and an almost religious rapture' believing in that instant they were freed.

That day – walk over to the **Radio Free Europe building** (**7**; p102) and the then parliament – the communist party leadership had resigned. On 3 December, the entire government stood down.

More demonstrations, a successful general strike, and negotiations between Civic Forum and the remaining communists followed 24 November. People taped up posters '*Havel na hrad*' ('Havel to the castle'). On 29 December they got their wish, sort of, when their man became Czechoslovak president – although Havel decided to govern from his own home!

>SNAPSHOTS

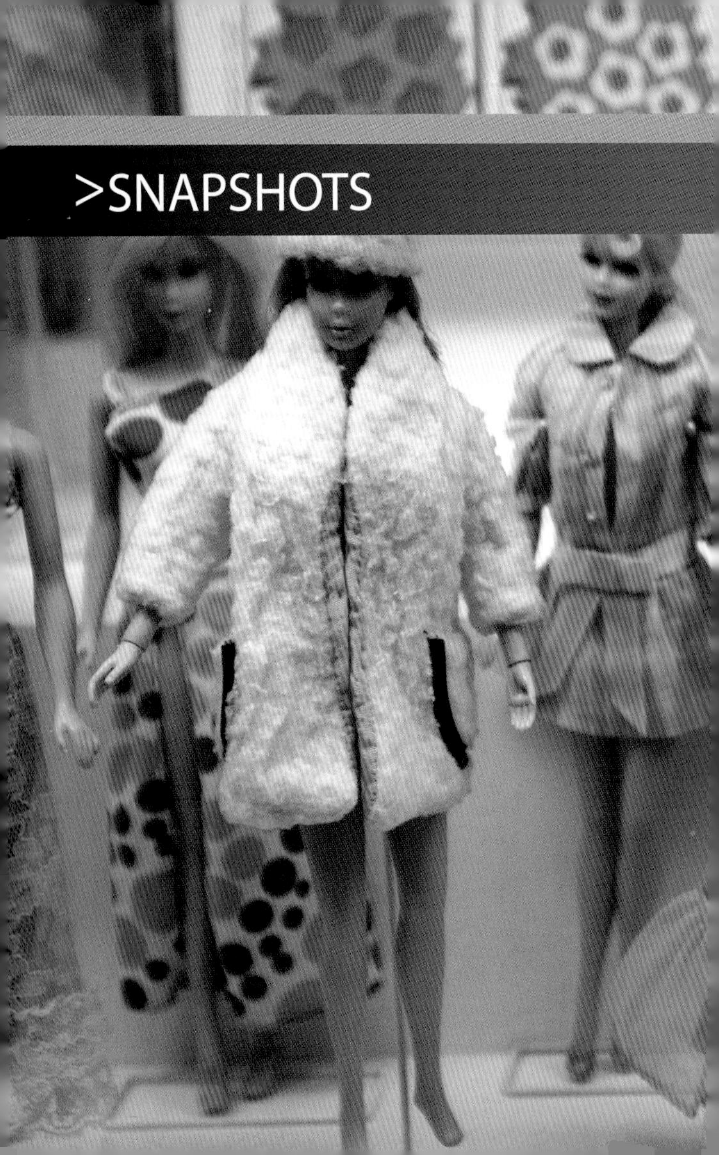

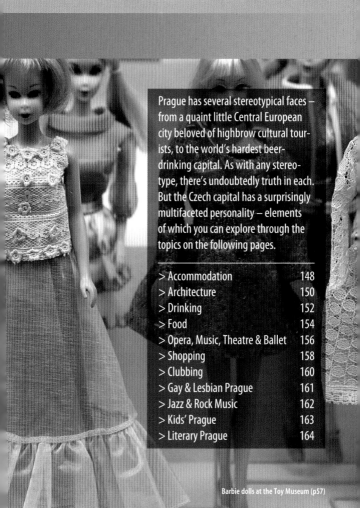

Prague has several stereotypical faces – from a quaint little Central European city beloved of highbrow cultural tourists, to the world's hardest beer-drinking capital. As with any stereotype, there's undoubtedly truth in each. But the Czech capital has a surprisingly multifaceted personality – elements of which you can explore through the topics on the following pages.

Barbie dolls at the Toy Museum (p57)

ACCOMMODATION

Early in 2007, central Prague did a count and suddenly realised it had more hotels (320) than streets (286). As a city that annually accommodates some four million tourists – more than three times its own population – it's hardly surprising that its property market has developed so furiously.

That doesn't always mean great bargains for visitors, however. The market is quite polarised, with fantastic five-star establishments charging just as much as in Western Europe, loads of cheap hostels and much less in the middle.

Luckily, as the many high-end hotels don't always fill their rooms, you can usually find a last-minute bargain on all the usual online booking sites. The Prague Information Service (www.pis.cz) sometimes has competitive prices. Other sites to try include www.hotels-of-prague.com and www.hotel.cz.

Malá Strana is a particularly scenic location in which to stay, but Prague's compact size means you can easily reach most sights regardless of where your hotel is. But if booking somewhere central, check your room is not facing a busy street.

The greatest excitement in the Prague hotel world in 2006 came when luxury chain Mandarin Oriental opened its first Central European hotel in Malá Strana. However, there were other significant developments. With its organic green, white and black rooms – and furry blood-orange triffids in its restaurant – Hotel Yasmin showed the march of the designer hotel was continuing (although, like many hotels in Prague, its service could be improved). And Prague now even has a designer hostel in the fabulous Czech Inn.

haystack.lonelyplanet.com

Need a place to stay? Find and book it at lonelyplanet.com. More than 59 properties are featured for Prague – each personally visited, thoroughly reviewed and happily recommended by a Lonely Planet author. From hostels to high-end hotels, we've hunted out the places that will bring you unique and special experiences. Read independent reviews by authors and other travellers, and get practical information including amenities, maps and photos. Then reserve your room simply and securely via Haystack – our online booking service. It's all at www.lonelyplanet.com/accommodation.

Even some of the city's grand old hotels are getting in on the act. Slightly shabby and long given over to school groups, the Art Nouveau Hotel Imperial (www.hotel-imperial.cz) is making a comeback in 2007 too.

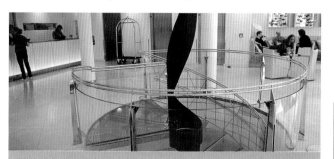

BEST LUXURY HOTELS
> Hotel Aria (www.ariahotel.net)
> Hotel Riverside (www.riverside prague.com)
> Le Palais Hotel (www.palaishotel.cz)
> Mandarin Oriental (www.mandarin oriental.com/prague)
> Radisson SAS (www.radissonsas.com)

MOST ROMANTIC HOTELS
> Hotel Alchymist (www.alchymist hotelresidence.com)
> Hotel Casa Marcello (www.casa -marcello.cz)
> Residence Nosticova (http://nosticova .com)
> U Krále Karla (www.romantichotels.cz)
> U Zlaté Studně (www.zlatastudna.cz)

GREAT PERSONAL SERVICE
> Arcadia (www.arcadiaresidence.com)
> Hostel Boathouse (www.aa.cz /boathouse)
> Hotel Julian (www.julian.cz)

BEST PETITE & BOUTIQUE
> Domus Henrici (www.domus-henrici.cz)
> Hotel Neruda (www.hotelneruda -praha.cz)
> Residence Nosticova (http://nosticova .com)
> Residence Santini (www.residence santini.com)

BEST DESIGNER DENS
> Andĕls Hotel (www.andelshotel.com)
> Hotel Josef (pictured above; www .hoteljosef.com)
> Hotel Maximilian (www.maximilian hotel.com)
> Hotel Yasmin (www.hotel-yasmin.cz)

BEST HOSTELS
> Czech Inn (www.czech-inn.com)
> Miss Sophie's (www.miss-sophies .com)

ARCHITECTURE

Prague is often called an 'open-air museum of architecture', and for once that's an epithet without exaggeration. Not only have the neighbour-hoods of Hradčany, Malá Strana, Staré Město and Nové Město jointly been granted Unesco World Heritage listing, nearly half of the city's 3500 build-ings are designated cultural monuments. The history of Prague – specifically its struggles for independence during repeated colonisations – is written in these buildings.

The earliest architecture is Romanesque from the later Přemysl princes of the 10th to 12th centuries. These Czech nobles, responsible for Prague Castle, commissioned buildings with heavy stone walls and small windows. However, perhaps the finest surviving example is an interior: namely that of St George's Basilica (p49) inside Prague Castle.

The Gothic architecture of the 13th to 16th centuries came about not just because of changing aesthetics, but because improvements in build-ing techniques allowed more streamlined structures. Typified by tall, pointed arches, spindly spires and ribbed vaults, this style is associated with a proud era in Czech history. This is when Charles IV made Prague the capital of the Holy Roman Empire and began commissioning monu-ments like St Vitus Cathedral and Charles Bridge (p56).

Conversely, Renaissance architecture in Prague is a reminder of Austrian rule. When the Habsburgs took over the Bohemian throne in the early 16th century they invited Italian designers and architects to create the Habsburg idea of a royal city. The Italians brought an enthusiasm for classical form, an obsession with grace and symmetry and a taste for exuberant decoration, all of which merged with local tastes in a distinc-tive 'Bohemian Renaissance' architecture. The devastating Great Fire in 1541 meant large swathes of Hradčany and Malá Strana were rebuilt in this Renaissance style. A much-used decorative technique of the time was *sgraffito*, a multilayered mural technique that creates a 3D effect, as on the façade of the Schwarzenberg Palace (p44).

Ironically – given how famous Prague is for its baroque architecture today – at the time it was a further way for the victorious Catholic Habsburgs to stamp their authority on Protestant-leaning Prague, after the inter-religious dispute of the Thirty Years' War (1618–48). Palaces, villas, town houses, ornamental gardens and, above all, churches were erected, especially in Malá Strana, during a baroque building spree. The most famous example is the green-domed Church of St Nicholas.

When Prague gained a measure of self-rule during the so-called Czech National Revival, major new public buildings were commissioned, including the neo-Renaissance National Theatre (p116) and the National Museum (p101). Architects then began to express their national aspirations through Art Nouveau (c 1899–1912), in the form of Municipal House (p75), Výstaviště (p133) and numerous apartment buildings in Vinohrady. Between 1910 and 1924 they then alighted uniquely on cubism (see p24).

The relatively elegant lines of 1920s Functionalism – as in Veletržní Palace (p133) and the Baťa store (p105) – gave way between the 1950s and '80s to fantastically ugly communist prefabs on the outskirts of the city. Perhaps because of this unedifying experience with modern architecture, Prazaks remain suspicious of new designs, which they fear might destroy the appearance of their quaint city. Although both are now much-loved fixtures on the skyline, there was initial resistance to the Dancing Building (p97) and the Kampa Museum (p57). Likewise, plans for a new National Library have meet with some cynicism (see the boxed text, p135).

For more, the Prague Information Service at the Old Town Hall (p185) publishes pamphlets to the Prague of various architectural eras – ie Gothic Prague, Renaissance Prague etc.

BEST GOTHIC
> Church of Our Lady Before Týn (p74)
> Church of Our Lady of the Snows (p97)
> Old Town Bridge Tower (p76)
> Powder Gate (p77)
> St Vitus Cathedral (p49)

BEST BAROQUE
> Loreta (p45)
> Church of St Nicholas (p57)
> Wallenstein Garden (p62)

Above Baroque houses on Nerudova

DRINKING

Delicious Czech beer is so famous it needs little introduction. On the other hand, it's a topic that can fill a book (try Evan Rail's *Good Beer Guide Prague & the Czech Republic*, 2007). The superlative taste of their *pivo* (beer) is one reason Czechs drink more per head than any other nation. They down an average 166L (293 pints) each a year, compared with 144L (253 pints) in runner-up Germany.

The country's soil is perfect for growing hops and brewing goes back more than 1000 years. But the big breakthrough came in the 19th century, when Plžen brewers developed the world's first lager – bottom-fermented and amber-coloured, unlike the dark beer then available. 'Pilsner' or 'Pils' became such a copycat hit that the Plžen brewery proprietarily labelled its beer Pilsner Urquell ('original source Pilsner' or *Plženský Prazdroj* in Czech).

Today, Pilsner Urquell remains a top Czech brand, but only Budvar remains Czech-owned. The boxed text, p91, explains why even major-brand beer sometimes tastes better here. However, many pubs produce their own microbrews and these are frequently the best treat.

Czech beer, like German, shuns chemicals and uses only water, hops, yeast and barley. In pubs, you'll find it in two main varieties – *světlé* (light), and *tmavy* or *černé* (dark). The *světlé* is a pale amber, modern lager. Dark beers are sweeter and more full-bodied.

Following a 17th-century custom, Czech beer is measured in 'degrees'. However, although that degree sign has become interchangeable with a percentage sign recently, it's not the amount of alcohol it measures. Rather, the Czech degree represents the malt extract used during brewing and the alcohol percentage is less than half this. Roughly, a 10-degree Czech beer contains 4% alcohol; a 12-degree beer has 4.5% to 5%.

Most draught beer is sold in 0.5L glasses, and you can usually order without saying anything; when the waiter approaches, just raise your thumb for one beer, thumb and index finger for two, etc. Even a nod will do. Your bill is recorded on a slip of paper on your table; don't write on it or lose it. As soon as your glass nears empty, another will appear. If you don't want more, place a beer-mat over your glass. To pay up and go, say *zaplatím* (I'll pay) or *zaplatíme* (we'll pay). It's normal to tip.

Of course, for many visitors, Prague is synonymous with another drink: absinth. That's been the case since the 1990s, when Czech drinks firm

Hills cleverly revived this long-banned, legendary and allegedly halluci-
natory 19th-century French–Swiss tipple. Today, however, the Swiss and
French have resumed production of genuine *'fée verte'*, and connoisseurs
have become pretty sniffy about replica 'Czechsinths'.

What's the difference? Most Czech brands (whether spelt absinth or
absinthe) use oil to mix the active ingredient, wormwood, into the liquid,
instead of properly distilling it. Czech absinths like Staroplzenecký also
omit anise, so taste awfully bitter. It's a complicated topic; see www
.feeverte.net, www.wormwoodsociety.org or www.absinthe.se. But,
whatever you're told, high thujone content, a 'Swiss recipe' or the spell-
ing 'absinthe' doesn't guarantee quality.

For most, the point of highly alcoholic absinth is to drink it rather than debate it. But if you're looking for more, experts do rate the pricey Czech Cami's
Absinthe Toulouse Lautrec (about 1100Kč, usually at Tesco on Národní třída,
p107). For imported French or Swiss absinthe, you might try the Roxy (p94).

Or you might prefer Becherovka. This herbal liqueur from Karlovy Vary
is a lot sweeter than absinth and delicious served with tonic (ask for a
'beton'). Conversely, the liquor Fernet is as bitter as absinth.

BEST-SELLING BEER BRANDS
> Budvar – malty and slightly sweet; *not* Budweiser!
> Gambrinus – this golden lager is the most popular beer locally
> Pilsner Urquell – the original and the most popular abroad
> Staropramen – slightly perfumed, local Prague brew (p61)
> Velké Popovice – this brewery's slightly bitter Kozel beer comes in dark and light varieties

BEST MICROBREWERIES
> Novoměstský pivovar (p112)
> Pivovar U Bulovky (p135)
> Pivovarský dům (p113)
> U Fleků (p113)
> U Medvídků (p91)

FOOD

Eating out in Prague is a seriously hit-and-miss affair, as the restaurant that doesn't regularly have an off night here seems to be a rare thing. Venues your friends, acquaintances and – heaven forfend – your guide-book swear by are never accident-proof. 'Many Prague restaurants can be horribly inconsistent,' *Prague Post* restaurant reviewer Dave Faries confirms when we ask him.

That said, culinary matters in Prague have improved immensely in the past decade. After all, at least restaurants have good nights now, a concept that was alien for many years after the communist period. International cuisines, from Afghan to Thai, Vietnamese and beyond, are easily as widespread as Czech cooking, while trendy, modern restaurant groups have injected much style into the proceedings. Check out Ambiente (www.ambi.cz), Kolkovna (www.kolkovna.cz) and Pravda Group (www .pravdagroup.cz/en/) for more restaurants than we could ever squeeze in. Prague's single most famous restaurant, Kampa Park, is run by the ever-growing Kampa Group (www.kampagroup.com).

Naturally, Czech fare is still widely consumed, although often in pubs as an afterthought to a beer. *Smažený sýr* (fried cheese) is a favourite pub snack, and *Pražska šunka* (cured and smoked Prague ham) is a popular appetiser, setting the tone for a meaty, fatty, creamy, salty and sugar-heavy cuisine.

The most ubiquitous Czech meal is *vepřová pečeně s knedlíky a kyselé zelí* (roast pork with dumplings and sauerkraut, often abbreviated to *vepřo-knedlo-zelo*). The pork is rubbed with salt and caraway seeds, and roasted long and slow. Bread dumplings look not unlike a sliced loaf and are slightly firm, to mop up the gravy.

Other staples include *vepřové kolínko* (pork knuckle), *svíčková na smetaně* (slices of marinated roast beef served with a sour-cream sauce garnished with lemon and cranberries) and *guláš* (a casserole of beef or pork in a tomato, onion and paprika gravy). Poultry – *kuře* (chicken) and *kachna* (duck) – is popular; *kapr* (carp) is the most traditional Czech fish. (Note the price of fish on the menu is sometimes not for the whole fish but per 100g.)

Despite all this, vegetarians find it pretty easy to eat in Prague today. A traditional dish you can try is *bramboráky* (potato pancakes), but you might want to check what stock is in any *Česneková polévka* (garlic soup). Of course, for *bezmasá jídla* (meat-free dishes) there are Italian, Asian and dedicated vegetarian restaurants, too.

When eating out in Prague, you might sometimes find your bill higher than expected. Stuff you'd take for granted elsewhere often comes at a price here – wave away items you didn't order or want, such as baskets of bread, condiments and, in more touristy places, 'free' drinks. Additionally, some places also charge for each diner (per cover or *couvert*) and others add a service charge to the bill – and still expect you to tip the usual 10% to 15%. Mostly, the above practices are just the way things are done, but unless the last – the service charge – is flagged on the menu, you could always try politely querying it. In very touristy places, it's always best to double-check your bill carefully, as sometimes 'mistakes' on the bill go beyond all these instances.

BEST CZECH
> U Maltézských Rytířů (p67)
> U Modré Kachničky (p67)

BEST FOR VIEWS
> Bellavista (p52)
> Cowboys terrace (p65)
> Kampa Park (p66)
> Hergetova Cihelná (p66)
> U Zlaté Studně (p67)

BEST FOR ROMANCE
> Kampa Park (p66)
> La Provence (p87)
> Pálffy Palác (p66)
> U Maltézských Rytířů (p67)
> U Modré Kachničky (p67)

MOST RELIABLE OPTIONS
(Not the kiss of death, we hope!)
> Ambiente (p123)
> Kogo (p110)
> Mozaika (p123)

OPERA, MUSIC, THEATRE & BALLET

As the city where Mozart chose to premiere *Don Giovanni,* and the birthplace of vaunted composers like Antonín Dvořák, Leoš Janáček and Bedřich Smetana, Prague has a long, proud tradition of opera and classical music. Add to that some beautiful theatres and very cheap tickets, and it's easy to see how the city has become a much-touted opera destination.

However, this reputation is only partially deserved. International experts say the standard of performance is quite variable – a message borne out by our own experience.

'It's untrue to say that they never do good things,' says John Allison, editor of the UK-based *Opera Today* magazine. 'However it is true to say that their opera is in a fairly troubled state,' he adds, referring to the loss of generous government funding in the post-communist era.

Opera is performed in three venues: the National Theatre (www .narodni-divadlo.cz), the Estates Theatre (run by the National Theatre) and the State Opera (www.opera.cz). Of those, Allison and other connoisseurs most highly rate the National Theatre. Despite some terrible management troubles in 2006–07, it still managed to pull off some critically well-received productions and its stunning auditorium is a perennial asset. The Estates Theatre, where Mozart himself conducted the *Don Giovanni* premiere, is also a beautiful, if somewhat compact, space. Its opera performances, however, are rarely aimed at the most discerning audiences.

Attending a classical concert is a somewhat better bet, especially if you book tickets for the Czech Philharmonic Orchestra at the Rudolfinum (www.ceskafilharmonie.cz). The Smetana Hall inside Municipal House (www.obecni-dum.cz) is architecturally stunning and atmospheric based on that alone, which might atone for the fact that the acoustics aren't that crisp. However, ticket-buyers should remain selective about which performances they choose. Not every troupe on stage is as talented as house musicians Prague Symphony Orchestra.

During festivals such as the Prague Spring (p27), international orchestras also appear in the city, making this one of the very best, albeit busy, times for the music fan to visit.

Throughout the year, theatre is excellent, but largely a closed book to non-Czech speakers. While the National Theatre subtitles its operas in English, it does not do the same for its plays. Fortunately, the one venue that provides such translation is also one of the city's youngest, funkiest and most vital stages, Švandovo Divadlo (www.svandovodivadlo.cz).

Generally, the cheapest theatre tickets are available in person from each venue's box office. They're usually not as expensive as those offered online even via the theatre's own website, and certainly not as costly as those through ticket agencies. Someone in the box office will usually speak a little English, and there are frequently same-day tickets available, or at least tickets for the next day's performances. If circumstances dictate you buy online, compare prices across the following: www.bohemiaticket.cz; www.ticketpro.cz; www.ticketsonline.cz.

Of course, the silent multimedia performances by Laterna Magika (www.laterna.cz) and related Black Light Theatre shows across town transcend all language barriers. However, it's fair to say that 21st-century Westerners find its charms somewhat of a mystery, and disappointing. One resident's warning – 'only go if you enjoy laughing yourself sick at tacky kitsch' – is probably a little harsh. But not much. If you're looking for something to entertain the kids, you're better off plumping for puppet theatre.

All of which leaves the ballet. Overall, this medium might not have as many fans as opera and classical music. Yet this is, surprisingly, the current hit on the Prague stage. Both the State Opera and National Theatre ballet troupes have been well reviewed and received recently.

BEST...
For opera National Theatre (p116)
For classical music Czech Philharmonic Orchestra at the Rudolfinum (p95)
For gawping at the ceiling Smetana Hall (p95)
For plays you can understand Švandovo Divadlo (p61)
Moves The State Opera Ballet (p117)
Avoided Black Light Theatre

Above Catch a classical concert at Smetana Hall, Municipal House (p75)

SHOPPING

Although its streets are lined with stores, Prague doesn't initially seem a particularly inspiring shopping destination. Bohemian crystal (or glassware), garnet jewellery and wooden marionettes are the most typical souvenirs. But the first two tend towards overly flamboyant and old-fashioned designs, while the third can be a bit twee. Additionally, there's a surfeit of amber and Russian *matryoshky* (nesting dolls), which have little to do with the city, plus an embarrassing rash of Kafka T-shirts and other souvenirs.

To compound the problem, Prague has been colonised in the past decade by international high-street chains, where the shopping isn't much cheaper or any different than at home. The fact that many such stores are housed in faceless shopping malls adds to the ennui.

Never fear, however. In such unpromising conditions, you really feel you've achieved something major when you alight on the city's real gems.

For a spot of mainstream shopping, Na příkopě is good. This long street boasts international chains from Benetton to Zara and some of the city's most famous malls.

For the most part, you can put your wallet away along Wenceslas Sq (not a bad idea anyway, considering the pickpocketing that goes on here). This famous boulevard is lined with high-street brands, frequently British, and a series of *Bankrot* (clearance sale) stores. Only Bat'a (p105), Promod (p107) and Palác Knih Neo Luxor (p107) deserve much of a look.

Instead, explore the Old Town's winding alleyways. Ritzy Pařížská is often called Prague's Champs Elysées and, although it's far smaller, it is lined with luxury brands like Cartier, Dolce & Gabbana, Hugo Boss and Ferragamo. Dlouhá, Dušní and surrounding streets house some original fashion boutiques, while even central Celetná contains a worthwhile stop or two.

Across town, you will still find old *antikvariáts* and junk stores harbouring Art Deco, Art Nouveau and other antiques. However, these days you're unlikely to find too many bargains in these.

OUR FAVOURITE CZECH SOUVENIRS

> Bottle of Becherovka (everywhere)
> Little Mole toy, cuddly or otherwise (Pohádka, p82, Rocking Horse Toy Shop, p51, Sparky's, p84)
> A set of Royal 9009 champagne glasses (Moser, p106)
> A knit or shirt subtly embroidered with a Czech lion (Bohème, p80)
> Painted Easter eggs (Havelská Market, p80, Easter Markets on Wenceslas Sq and any branch of Manufaktura, p82)
> Ornate gingerbread figures made from medieval moulds (Manufaktura, Mostecká branch, p63)
> Jiří Pecl sperm-shaped teaspoons (Modernista, p82)
> Maxim Velčovský 'Pure' plastic-cup-shaped, barcoded procelain beaker (Qubus, p84, Modernista, p82)
> *Czech 100 Design Icons* book (Museum of Decorative Arts, p76, Veletržní Palace, p133)
> Book of Josef Sudek or Josef Koudelka photography (Museum of Decorative Arts, p76, Veletržní Palace, p133)
> *David Černý: The Fucking Years* book (Žižkov Tower, p121 – if you ask, persistently)
> Chic 495Kč leather gloves (Christmas Market, náměstí Republiky)

Top Pick up a souvenir at Havelská Market (p80)

CLUBBING

No-one would come to Prague for serious, cutting-edge clubbing, particularly when hipper Berlin is so near. There's plenty of nightlife in the Czech capital, and big-name bands and DJs put in the occasional appearance, but this is not a place for chasing the latest European trends. Instead, it's a destination for letting down your hair and revelling in some unpretentious fun.

It's true that in the more fashionable venues (eg Mecca), VIP tickets are sold and there are roped-off VIP areas. At the same time, however, door staff never seem to enforce any dress code, so wear what you like. Some clubs ban large groups of men who look like stag parties, but the spirit of the city's widespread sex industry rubs off slightly on even the most respectable clubs (ie, there's loads of cruising and picking up people here).

Musically, dance clubs mostly cater to partying students and tourists weaned on MTV. Some have a particular penchant for '80s and '90s video evenings, where you'll be guaranteed to hear such 'delights' as Bon Jovi ('Living on a Prayer'), Depeche Mode ('Feel the Silence') and even Europe (remember 'The Final Countdown'?). Otherwise happy house predominates.

Fortunately, there are a few alternative music clubs, DJ bars and 'experimental' venues. The Roxy and Žižkov's Palác Akropolis are also much loved.

BEST FOR HOUSE & TECHNO
> Infinity (p127)
> Mecca (p138)
> Misch Masch (p138)
> Radost FX (p128)
> Roxy (p94)

BEST FOR '80S & '90S EVENINGS
> Futurum (weekends; p61)
> Lucerna Music Bar (weekends; p115)

BEST FOR BRITPOP
> M1 Lounge (p93)

BEST GRUNGY DJ BARS
> Cross Club (p137)
> Palác Akropolis (p127)
> Wakata (p138)

BEST AFTERPARTY VENUES
> Le Clan (p127)
> M1 Lounge (p93)

BEST FOR HIP-HOP & R&B
> Chateau/L'Enfer Rouge (p93)
> Misch Masch (p138)
> Radost FX (Thu & Sat; p128)

GAY & LESBIAN PRAGUE

SNAPSHOTS

Prague has a medium-sized gay and lesbian scene, which locals describe as having picked up enormously recently. Specifically, in the past two to three years a definite 'gay quarter' (or 'gaybourhood') has developed, just out of central Prague in Vinohrady. With top venues Valentino, Termix and Saints leading the way, there are now at least 10 venues all within 10 minutes of each other, in and around the metro station of Náměstí Míru.

According to one regular, the scene is very easy-going. There's no 'face control', or dress code at the door, and even the top venues don't charge entrance fees. To all intents and purposes, homophobia barely exists in Prague. (Czechs are too laid-back to be prejudiced, one resident suggests!) There's also no problems with rampaging British stag parties, which are fewer in number these days, but who stick to the centre in any case.

Although things differ from bar to bar, the scene is very mixed between Czechs and foreigners. For English speakers, an excellent first stop is Saints (www.praguesaints.cz), which runs a gay travel and accommodation service and maintains an up-to-date website with an interactive map of the scene.

TOP GAY CLUBS
> Friends (pictured right; p89)
> Saints (p126)
> Termix (p128)
> Valentino (p128)

TOP GAY NIGHTS
> Lollypop, 1st Fri of the month, Radost FX (p128)
> Occasional 'Pink Stars' party, Celnice (p91)

BEST LESBIAN NIGHTS
> Thursdays, Saints (p126)
> Monthly, Friends (p89)

JAZZ & ROCK MUSIC

SNAPSHOTS

The city in which former US president Bill Clinton revealed his skill with a saxophone in the 1990s already had a deep-rooted jazz scene. Czechs figured prominently in European jazz circles from the 1920s until the 1948 communist coup d'état, and even under communism the art form survived. Prague's first professional jazz club, Reduta, opened during the less censorial atmosphere of the 1960s, although these days it's a little more 'establishment'.

There is still a jazz sensibility at large in the city today. Perhaps the venue that most upholds the free-form, improvisational spirit of the music is the tiny U Malého Glena. The somewhat more commercial Agharta Jazz Centrum hosts gigs by local and international musicians.

As to pop, there are a few local bands worth seeing. New York–style indie rockers Sunshine are probably the only ones even vaguely known abroad, but there's also the electro-pop Nihilists, folky 'Czech Pogues' Čechomor, spacy Sunflower Caravan and Smiths-influenced Southpaw. However, on a short break it's more useful to know which international acts might be touring. Websites like www.praguepost.com, www.prague.tv and www.expats.cz have information on upcoming events. At www.ticketpro.cz you can not only checking out what's happening, but buy tickets online, too.

BEST FOR JAZZ
> Agharta Jazz Centrum (pictured right; p92)
> Dinitz Café (p86)
> Reduta (p116)
> U Malého Glena (p69)

BEST FOR ROCK
> Abaton (p137)
> Lucerna Music Bar (p115)
> Palác Akropolis (p127)
> T-Mobile Arena (HC Sparta Praha, p137)
> Vagon (p117)

KIDS' PRAGUE

Like a city they might see in a bedtime picture book, Prague is a charming destination for children. They'll be enchanted by Prague Castle and its Toy Museum (even if they can't touch its exhibits; pictured below) and get a kick out of the Miniatures Museum. Riding a tram and looking in toyshops can also entertain younger visitors.

Prague has many gardens for taking a break. There are playground areas at Letná (p132) and on Children's Island (Děstký ostrov; Map p61). The Wallenstein Garden, with its weird stalactite wall, will intrigue all ages, but one of the best places for children is Petřín Hill. Not only will they enjoy the funicular ride; there's a mirror maze up here, too.

Kids might not enjoy spending much time in the city's more crowded areas of Staré or Nove Město, but they will enjoy the puppet theatres. Although not many Czechs take their children out to eat, several restaurants including Kogo (p110) offer high chairs. Oliva (p104) has a lovely children's area. Despite being achingly hip, Hot (p109) also promises that children under 12 eat for free (at least at the time of writing; call to check).

TOP SIGHTSEEING WITH KIDS
> Prague Castle & Toy Museum (p10)
> Miniatures Museum (p45)
> Nový Svět Quarter (p46)
> Petřín Hill (p59)
> Vyšehrad (p22)

BEST KIDS' THEATRES
> Minor Theatre (p116)
> Rise Loutek (p94)

SNAPSHOTS

LITERARY PRAGUE

The late Alan Levy, former editor of the *Prague Post,* dubbed Prague 'the left bank of the 1990s' early in that decade, and plenty of other romantics – many American – were thinking the same. This stirring notion was forged by writers' prominent role in the Czechoslovak anti-communist resistance, from Charta 77 onwards, and by seeing playwright Válav Havel in the presidential hot seat. Aiding and abetting the Paris myth were the many undergraduates thumbing Milan *(Unbearable Lightness of Being)* Kundera and Ivan *(Love and Garbage)* Klima in the early 1990s.

Many young hopefuls, also lured by cheap costs, expatriated themselves here to pursue dreams of a writing career. A decade on, however, no-one seems to have produced the 'Great Prague Novel' nor spawned a major literary movement. (This despite Czech writer Jáchym Topol's award-winning *City, Sister, Silver* in 2000.)

What all the fuss did leave Prague was a brace of excellent, community-minded English-language bookshops, where you can still see locally based and international writers perform readings.

And of course, there's an earlier literary legacy – of Jan Neruda, Jaroslav Hašek, Franz Kafka and Bohumil Hrabal (see p171). Neruda is best revisited around Nerudova (p59) and in Vyšehrad Cemetery (p22). Hrabal loved the pubs U Zlatého Tygra (p92) and U Pinkasů (p113); Hašek loved any pub. For more on Kafka, start at p17.

BEST ENGLISH-LANGUAGE BOOKSHOPS
> Anagram (p79)
> Big Ben (p79)
> Globe (pictured right; p108)
> Shakespeare & Sons (p122)

BEST LITERARY FESTIVAL
> Prague Writers' Festival (p28)

>BACKGROUND

Wenceslas Sq (p103)

BACKGROUND

HISTORY

After centuries of turbulent history, Prague has enjoyed a steady rhythm in the past nearly 20 years. There has been some trouble at the top, with a stalemate in national government and rumours of corruption in city hall. There are also (thankfully decreasing) hordes of British and Irish stag parties still running through the city. But that's all fairly manageable after the defenestrations, burnings at the stake, fire, floods, war, occupation, Soviet-backed coup and revolutions of the past.

IN THE BEGINNING

The name Bohemia, still used to describe the western Czech Republic, comes from Celtic tribe the Boii, who lived in the area that later became Prague around 400 BC. Later, in the 6th century, two Slavic tribes arrived – with the 'Czechs' building a wooden fortress near the current castle, and the Zličani settling at Vyšehrad (p22).

However, it wasn't until the 9th-century Přemyslid dynasty that Czech history really got going. The Přemysls not only built the earliest section of today's Prague Castle (p10) in the 9th century, but also included one Václav, or Wenceslas, of 'Good King' carol fame (see the boxed text, opposite).

THE GOLDEN AGE

Even this early in history, Germans had their eye on Czech territory. In 950 Holy Roman Emperor Otto I invaded Bohemia, after which it essentially became Otto's fiefdom, run by the Přemysls as a client state.

It was only in the 14th century, after the Přemysls died out and Prague came under the direct rule of Holy Roman Emperor Charles IV (1316–78), that the city blossomed. During this 'golden age', Charles – whose mother was Czech – elevated Prague's official status and went on a building spree, founding the New Town (Nové Město; p96) and adding St Vitus Cathedral to the castle. Charles Bridge (p56) and Charles University (Map pp72–3, D4) also owe their existence to him.

One of that university's rectors, Jan Hus, led the 15th-century Hussite movement, which challenged the Catholic Church and its corruption, as Martin Luther later did in Germany. Hus was famously burned at the stake in 1415 for his reformist 'heresy', but his death kicked off decades of internecine fighting that eventually put Hussites in charge for several

GOOD KING WENCESLAS LOOKED OUT...
English clergyman John Mason Neale wrote the Christmas carol 'Good King Wenceslas' in 1853, inspired by the tale of a page and his master taking food and firewood to the poor on a freezing Boxing Day. However, Neale was either mistaken or exaggerated. Wenceslas (Václav in Czech) wasn't a king, but the duke of Bohemia.

In that capacity, from 925–29, Wenceslas helped bring Christianity to Czech lands. Now Czechs' chief patron saint, his image pops up across town, from St Vitus Cathedral (p49) to the Wenceslas Statue (p105).

Despite his piety, however, Wenceslas came to an unfortunate end, murdered by his brother Boleslav for cosying up to neighbouring Germans.

decades. There's a statue of Hus in the Old Town Sq, while victorious Hussite military commander Jan Žižka is commemorated in Žižkov (p121).

HABSBURG RULE
In 1526 Czech lands came under the rule of the Austrian Habsburgs. There was a honeymoon period when the eccentric Rudolf II temporarily moved his court from Vienna to Prague. However, with the Reformation in full swing in Europe, tensions between Catholic Habsburgs and reformist Czechs inevitably surfaced. In 1618 Bohemian rebels threw two Catholic councillors from a Prague Castle window (see the boxed text, p45), sparking the Europe-wide Thirty Years' War (1618–1648). At home the Bohemian rebellion was savagely crushed. Following a defeat of the Czech nobility in 1620 at the Battle of White Mountain (Bílá Hora, the terminus of today's tram 22), the Czechs lost their independence for nearly 300 years.

NATIONAL REVIVAL & FIRST REPUBLIC
The Habsburg empire became the Austro-Hungarian Empire, and like many smaller ethnicities corralled into that colonial stable, Czechs longed for independence. During the 19th century there was a so-called National Revival, in which the desire for a stand-alone state manifested itself in artistic expression (see Books, p171, and Music, p174). A distinctive architecture also took form (see p150).

In 1861 nationalist Czechs defeated German-speaking candidates in Prague council elections, though the shrinking German minority still wielded influence. But it was the Austro-Hungarian defeat in WWI that

BACKGROUND

saw Czechs and Slovaks granted their dearest wish. Finally, on 28 October 1918, Czechoslovakia was born, under the presidency of writer and philosopher Tomáš Masaryk.

WAR & OCCUPATION

Sadly, the so-called First Republic lasted just 20 years before Nazis rolled in to 'protect' the largely German-speaking Sudetenland in 1938, and in the following year occupied Bohemia and Moravia.

Prague suffered little physical damage during WWII. However, the Nazis infamously crushed the Czech resistance – and Lidice village – in retaliation for the Prague assassination of Reichsprotektor Reinhard Heydrich (see the boxed text, p102).

COMMUNISM & RESISTANCE

Not content with a controlling position in the post-war coalition after the 1946 elections, the Czech Communist Party staged a coup d'etat in 1948, backed by the Soviet Union. The next decade and a half saw widespread political persecution – enumerated by the Memorial to the Victims of Communism in Malá Strana (p58).

In the late 1960s national Communist Party leader Alexander Dubček loosened the reins slightly under the banner of 'socialism with a human face'. There was a cultural resurgence in literature, theatre and film, led by the likes of Milan Kundera, Bohumil Hrabal, Václav Havel and Miloš For-

THE JEWS OF PRAGUE

Jews began living in Prague in the 9th century, forced into a walled ghetto from the 13th. Frequently persecuted by the authorities, they did enjoy golden periods under Emperor Rudolf II (r 1576–1612), Mayor Mordechai Maisel (1528–1601) and Rabbi Löw (1525–1609, see p78) and also after helping repel invading Swedes on Charles Bridge in 1648 at the end of the Thirty Years' War.

Emancipation – or legal equality – came from 1848, when the ghetto walls were torn down and the Jewish quarter renamed Josefov in honour of the emperor of the time. As wealthy Jews moved out the area slid into squalor. Between 1896 and 1910 this 'slum' was cleared, split down the middle by Pařížká (Paris Ave) and rebuilt in Art Nouveau style.

The community itself was all but eliminated by the Nazis, and today only some 6000 Jews remain in Prague. It's said the Nazis preserved the synagogues of today's Jewish Museum (p77) because, chillingly, they wanted to build a museum of an extinct race.

man. The Soviet regime crushed this 'Prague Spring' on 20 August 1968, using Warsaw Pact tanks, and Dubček was replaced by the orthodox Gustáv Husák.

VELVET REVOLUTION

In January 1977 a document called Charta 77 was signed by 243 intellectuals and artists, including Václav Havel. This public demand for basic human rights became an anticommunist tenet for dissidents, who kept campaigning for years.

On 17 November 1989 a violent police attack on a peaceful Prague rally prompted the mass public support the resistance needed, by sparking continuous public demonstrations on Wenceslas Sq, and a 750,000-strong rally on Letná plain (25–26 November).

A group led by Havel procured the government's resignation on 3 December, and 26 days later he was the new leader. The 'Velvet Revolution' – named for its peaceful nature and the inspirational role of psychedelic '60s band the Velvet Underground – had succeeded (see Art & Politics, p171, and the Velvet Revolution Walking Tour, p144).

VELVET DIVORCE

The smoothness of both the revolution and the initial transition to a free market made Czechs the poster children for the post-communist world in the early 1990s. But if everyone was hoping for a fairy-tale ending, it never completely arrived.

The Slovak and Czech nations did divorce peacefully on 1 January 1993, when Prague became capital of the new Czech Republic with Havel as president. However, subsequent years have been marred by a highly unpopular, and unstable, power-sharing arrangement between left-wing and right-wing politicians. Havel stepped down in 2003 and Václav Klaus took the presidential seat. Splits in the government grew even worse after elections in 2006, when attempts to form a three-party coalition and then a minority government led to recurring political stalemate and crisis.

The year 2002 was a bad one for Prague, when it suffered its worst flood in centuries that August, with large areas underwater, historic buildings destroyed and the metro system inoperable for months. However, more than five years later, having joined the EU in 2004, Prague looks as good as it ever did. Today, a regular income from tourism and a solid industrial base keep the mood relatively buoyant.

LIFE AS A PRAZAK

According to Swiss bank UBS, Prague has the best standard of living in Central and Eastern Europe. But life in Prague, as you as a visitor will experience it, is still out of reach to many working-class Prazaks. There is a growing Czech middle class, people with good jobs who are starting to embrace Prague's restaurants and clubs just as enthusiastically as they're latching on to loans and credit cards. However, this group is still relatively small and, according to a Czech Statistical Office (CSU) survey conducted in 2007, many households still face difficulties covering their outgoings.

According to other official figures, up to a third of household income can go on groceries. Therefore, the rest of the economy is disproportionately driven by tourists and the sizable expat community, the latter of which accounts for 7.6% of Prague's population (CSU, 2006). Still, Prazaks have it good compared to their compatriots: they earn a quarter more than the national average. Indeed, like most capital-city dwellers, they're sometimes lambasted by their countryfolk for their snooty ways.

Some visitors, too, find Prazaks a tad brusque. Certainly it's not standard to wish people 'have a nice day' in restaurants, bars and shops, particularly in the busiest tourists districts. Don't take it personally; that's just the way it is. (And sometimes they can be surprisingly friendly.) Czechs can seem impassive if you don't know them, but if you were to stay longer you'd find there's a definite strain of playful, sardonic humour that runs through the culture.

One thing they're always willing to spend their hard-earned money on is beer. They're the world's largest consumers of it (see p152), and even on a short trip you might see them letting down their hair if you venture into a local pub. Educated and generally older Prazaks also

DID YOU KNOW?

> Population 1.2 million
> Inflation 2.8%
> Prague unemployment 3.5%
> Czech unemployment 7.7%
> Prague average monthly wage 25,000Kč (€895)
> Czech average monthly wage 20,000Kč (€715)

splash out when they can on a trip to the theatre or opera. Here, as in the city's clubs and restaurants, Czechs demonstrate that they're not sticklers for the latest fashions. At the theatre and opera, dress will be smart but not overly formal, and elsewhere around town you'll rarely feel underdressed.

ARTS & POLITICS

One of the Czech Republic's great appeals to idealists and dreamers is the way literature, music and film have helped drive political resistance to unwelcome regimes – and actually won.

In neighbouring Poland it was gruff, tough shipyard workers who took battering rams to the communist monolith in the 1980s under the Solidarity banner. In Czechoslovakia it was bohemian novelists, artists and intellectuals who fomented dissent in smoky beer halls and at music gigs, published underground *samzidat* manuscripts, went to jail and poked fun at their totalitarian leaders and eventually outsmarted them.

Where else could a president seriously attribute his ascendancy to the inspiration of the Velvet Underground (for heaven's sakes), as avid fan Václav Havel once declared to the band's singer Lou Reed?

The Czech nation's tendency to define itself in word and song is typical for people absorbed into larger empires. Just as the 19th-century National Revival attempted to establish an independent identity within the wider Austro-Hungarian Empire, 20th-century Czech works criticised (obliquely or otherwise) the Soviet regime.

BOOKS

After centuries in which German reigned as Habsburg-controlled Prague's official tongue, modern Czech literature emerged during the nationalist movement of the 19th century. Since then, Czechs have forged a formidable literary tradition.

Folk-tale collector and novelist Božena Němcová, author of 1855's *Babička* (Grandma), was one of the first to publish in the local language and is now considered 'the mother of Czech prose'. However, other patriotic writers like Jan *(Tales of the Little Quarter)* Neruda soon followed.

Karel Čapek's sci-fi play *RUR* (Rossum's Universal Robots, 1920) is remembered mainly just for popularising the word 'robot'. However, Jaroslav Hašek's landmark novel *The Good Soldier Švejk* (1922) remains

TOP READS

> *The Good Soldier Švejk*, Jaroslav Hašek (1922) – laugh-out-loud funny and a genuine insight into the national character, this essential read follows a bumbling Czech conscript in the WWI Austrian army. But is Švejk really stupid or just playing dumb to thwart authority?

> *I Served the King of England*, Bohumil Hrabal (1971) – this fantastic (in all senses of the word) tale follows the rise of waiter Ditie to millionaire hotel owner and Nazi husband, before a relieved return to poverty in a short 'memoir' mirroring Czech history.

> *The Trial*, Franz Kafka (1925) – Kafka plumbs deep-seated human fears having 'Josef K' arrested and tried for a crime that's never explained to him. Nightmarish bureaucracy and existential guilt are crowned with one of the best openers in world literature (see p17).

widely read; it's a deceptively light romp with much between the lines about the Czech character and condition.

Hašek's device of humorously weaving an allegorical, historical tale around a Czech everyman isn't unique. Writer Bohumil Hrabal also uses the technique in classics like *Closely Observed Trains* (1965) and *I served the King of England* (1971). The latter even verges on magical realism.

Before WWII Czech literature was dominated by the avant-garde movement, including poet Jaroslav Seifert, who would go on to win the Nobel Prize for Literature in 1984.

After the 1968 Soviet invasion, writers were driven either into exile or underground. Milan Kundera, for example, produced *The Unbearable Lightness of Being* (1984) from his adopted homeland of France.

Others remaining in the Czech Republic, such as Ivan Klima (*The Spirit of Prague* and *Love and Garbage*), were banned and before 1989 could only circulate their works clandestinely via *samzidat* manuscripts. In between spells in prison, dissident poet and playwright Václav Havel (*Garden Party*, *The Memorandum*) led the Charta 77 group in publicly demanding basic human rights from the communist leadership.

Ironically, Prague's most celebrated pen-wielding son didn't even write in Czech, but came from the city's German-speaking Jewish community. Franz Kafka (*The Castle*, *Metamorphosis*) wasn't well known when he died in 1924. However, his friend Max Brod ignored instructions to burn Kafka's then-unpublished works and *The Trial* is now frequently voted the most influential 20th-century novel.

FILMS

Little Prague is home to Barrandov, the largest film studio in Europe. Opened in 1933, it forms the cornerstone of a proud homegrown industry. Several of the best Czech films can be bought abroad on video or DVD, but being in Prague is your chance to delve deeper; start at Kino Světozor (p115).

As an Oscar-winner, *Closely Observed Trains* (*Ostre sledované vlaky*, aka *Closely Watched Trains*, 1966) usually tops the list. A product of the Czech New Wave, it was the first collaboration between leading director Jiří Menzel and writer Bohumil Hrabal, based on the latter's gently humorous coming-of-age tale of a young train-station guard's very separate struggles with premature ejaculation and Nazis during WWII. Menzel and Hrabal also worked together on the charming *Larks on a String* (*Skrivánci na niti,* 1990). In 2006, nine years after Hrabal's death, Menzel finally brought the author's *I served the King of England* to the big screen – sadly not entirely successfully.

Miloš Forman was another director to emerge from the 1960s Czech New Wave. Now an American citizen, he's generally known for *One Flew Over the Cuckoo's Nest, Amadeus* and *The People vs Larry Flynt*. However, early Czech productions like *Black Peter* (*Černý Petr*, aka *Peter & Paula,* 1963) and *Loves of a Blonde* (*Lásky jedné plavovlásky,* 1965) remain popular here.

Mad genius Jan Švankmajer is in a league of his own, combining puppets, stop-motion animation and live action in surreal retellings of Goethe, Lewis Carroll, the Brothers Grimm, Edgar Allen Poe, the Marquis de Sade and more. A white rabbit wields scissors in a little girl's face, huge marionettes run down Prague streets, a boy fashioned from a tree stump comes to life and eats everything in his wake, etc, etc, in an enormous body of work including *Alice* (*Neco z Alenky,* 1988), *Faust* (1994), *Conspirators of Pleasure* (*Spiklenci slasti,* 1996), *Greedy Guts* (*Otesánek,* aka *Little Otik,* 2000) and *Lunacy* (*Sílení,* 2005). Švankmajer is widely cited as an influence on Tim Burton and Terry Gilliam; check him out on YouTube.

In the post–Cold War era the most successful Czech film has been the Oscar-winning *Kolja* (1996), a somewhat sentimental tale about a Russian boy raised by a Czech bachelor. Meanwhile Barrandov has become a popular hub for international blockbusters – from Tom Cruise's *Mission: Impossible* to Angelina Jolie, Morgan Freeman and James McAvoy's cartoon-inspired action movie *Wanted* – offering good star-spotting opportunities around Prague.

MUSIC

Details on listening to music in Prague are found on p156 and p162. However, it's worth noting that music here has also frequently been political. Indeed, 'in music is the life of the Czechs', claimed 19th-century composer Bedřich Smetana, at the laying of the foundation stone for the Prague National Theatre in 1868.

Smetana and contemporaries Antonín Dvořák and Leos Janaček were all concerned to create specifically Czech classical music, unlike their German-influenced predecessors. So while Janaček incorporated Slovak folk tunes and the cadences of spoken Czech into his famous *Sinfonietta* and other works, Smetana saluted his virtual country with a cycle of six symphonies entitled *Má vlast* (*My Fatherland*). Most people would instantly recognise the first, *Vltava,* a big, swelling echo of Prague's river that has been frequently co-opted by Hollywood.

Janaček's work is – patriotically – heard in the film version of Kundera's *The Unbearable Lightness of Being* (1988, starring Daniel Day-Lewis and Juliette Binoche). Dvořák's most famous piece is his *New World* symphony, which astronaut Neil Armstrong took on humankind's first trip to the moon.

While Prague's jazz scene remained largely undisturbed by the communist authorities, rock and pop was considered subversive and driven underground. In such a closed environment, a Velvet Underground album that arrived in Prague in 1968 electrified the dissident movement, especially after a group called the Plastic People of the Universe began covering the American group's songs (badly, by all accounts, but that's not the point). The Plastic People insisted they weren't activists, but when they were banned and arrested in 1976, they became a focal point for the resistance movement.

Tom Stoppard's 2006 hit play *Rock 'n' Roll* looked back at rock music's role in the anti-communist Czechoslovak resistance. Meanwhile, the ageing Plastic People still play across Prague; you might catch them at Vagon (p117).

PAINTING & PHOTOGRAPHY

Probably the three Czech artists best known abroad are painter Alfons Mucha and photographers Josef Sudek and Josef Koudelka. Alfons Mucha was one of the founding fathers of Art Nouveau, and is well displayed at the Mucha Museum (p101). Neo-romantic Sudek (1896–1976) was called 'the poet of Prague' for his nightscapes of the city. Today, his studio (www.sudek-atelier.cz) generally shows other photographers, but one or two of his silver gelatin prints are displayed at the Museum of Decorative Arts (p76). Koudelka (1938–) became famous for his photos of Roma, of Soviet tanks crushing the Prague Spring in 1968, and of landscapes. He lives in France and there's criminally little on him in Prague, apart from special exhibitions. However, there is the chance to learn about other Czech artists, particularly at the Kampa Museum (p57) and Veletržní Palace (p133).

DIRECTORY
TRANSPORT
ARRIVAL & DEPARTURE
AIR
Prague-Ruzyně Airport (☎ 220 113 314; www.prg.aero) is 17km west of the city centre. There are two international passenger terminals – Terminal North 2 is for flights to/from Schengen Agreement countries (most continental EU nations, plus Switzerland, Iceland and Norway), and Terminal North 1 is for flights to/from non-Schengen countries (including the UK, Ireland and non-European destinations).

Both arrival halls have exchange counters, ATMs, accommodation and car-hire agencies, public-transport information desks, taxi services and 24-hour left-luggage counters.

Getting Into Town
See the table below for the main methods for reaching the centre of town.

Beware of hailing other taxis at the airport; if they're not AAA you might get ripped off.

Private car services are also available, including **Airport Cars** (☎ 220 113 892; 650Kč for up to 4 passengers; 30min or more during rush hour) and **Prague Airport Shuttle** (www.prague-airport-shuttle.com; 600Kč for up to 4 passengers; 30min or more during rush hour).

BUS
Few short-break travellers will arrive in Prague by bus, unless

	Bus 119	Cedaz Shuttlebus
Pick-up point	TN1 & TN2	TN1 & TN2
Drop-off point	Dejvická metro station	Dejvická metro station, then náměstí Republiky
Duration	15min; services run every 20min 4.15am–midnight	15–25min; services run half-hourly 6am–9pm
Cost	20Kč; unusually for Prague, this bus stop has a ticket machine	60Kč (Dejvická); 90Kč (Dejvická plus metro ride or náměstí Republiky)
Other	Luggage ticket might be needed (see the boxed text, p178). This service is notorious for pickpockets in high season.	Cedaz shuttle buses will also take you directly to your hotel, from 480 Kč
Contact	www.dp-praha.cz	☎ 220 114 296; www.cedaz.cz

making a connection from a low-cost flight to surrounding airports like Bratislava. For these travellers, services arrive in Prague at **Florenc bus station** (Map pp72-3, H3; ☎ 12 999; www.jizdnirady.cz; Křižíkova 4, Karlín). The best bus company is **Student Agency** (☎ 224 999 666; www.studentagency.cz), with cheap fares and comfy new coaches with onboard stewards and movies. The website is Czech only, but phone operators speak English.

TRAIN
International trains arrive at either **Praha-Holešovice** (Map p131, E1; eg trains from Berlin, Bratislava, Budapest and Vienna, plus some from Warsaw) or the main station, **Praha hlavní nádraží** (Map pp98–9, G2; eg most services from Cologne, Nu-

remberg and Warsaw). Both have international booking windows with English-speaking staff, hotel booking services and a dedicated metro station on line C (the red line) providing quick access into town. Note that hlavní nádraží is undergoing redevelopment until 2009, so be prepared for some building work.

Timetable information is available online at www.idos.cz (English button in the bottom right-hand corner).

GETTING AROUND
Prague has an excellent integrated public transport system (www.dpp.cz) of metro, trams, buses and night trams, but when you're moving around the compact old town or the castle area, you might find it

AAA Taxi	Bus 100	Airport Express (AE) bus
TN1 & TN2	TN1 & TN2	TN1 & TN2
By arrangement	Zličín metro station	Dejvická metro station, then Praha-Hoselovice train station
30min, more during rush hour	15min; services run every 15-30min 5.40am-11.54pm	15min to Dejvická, 35min to Holesovice; services run every 30min 9.15am-10.15pm
350-550Kč depending on final destination	20Kč	30Kč to Dejvická, 45Kč to Holesovice
	Useful for those needing metro line B. Note luggage ticket might be needed (see the boxed text, p178).	
☎ 14 014; www.aaataxi.cz	www.dp-praha.cz	

more convenient and scenic to use your feet. If you're using the metro system, bank on about one or two minutes per metro stop. Times between tram stops are posted at each stop and on www.dpp.cz.

TRAVEL PASSES

You must buy a ticket (jízdenka) before boarding, and then validate it by punching it in the little yellow machine in the metro station lobby or on the bus or tram when you begin your journey. Checks by inspectors are frequent and there's a 900Kč fine for travelling without a time-stamped ticket, reduced to 500Kč if you pay on the spot. There's also a 50Kč fine for not having a luggage ticket (see the boxed text, below).

You'll need coins for ticket machines at metro stations and major tram stops, but can pay for tickets with notes at newsstands, Trafiky snack shops, PNS newspaper kiosks, hotels, PIS tourist information offices (see p185) and most metro station ticket offices.

Ticket options are listed in the boxed text, below. Day or three-day passes are easiest, but make sure you'll be travelling enough to need one. Kids under six travel free.

METRO

The metro operates from 5am to midnight. There are three lines: line A (green) runs from Dejvická in the northwest to Depo Hostivař in the east; line B (yellow) runs from Zličín in the southwest to Černý Most in the northeast; and

Ticket type	Cost	Validity	Luggage ticket needed?
Single transfer	20/10Kč per adult/ child aged 6-15yr	For unlimited transfers over 75min (if stamped 5am-8pm weekdays); otherwise for 90min on all transport	Yes, 10Kč for large suitcases or backpacks (above 25cm x 45cm x 70cm)
Short-hop	14/7Kč per adult/child	For 20min on buses and trams, or for up to 30min & five stations on the metro. Only metro line transfers permitted. Invalid on Petřín funicular or night trams & buses.	Yes; as above
24hr	80Kč	On all transport - tram, metro, bus, Petřín funicular, night tram & night bus	No
3-day	220Kč	As above	No
7-day	280Kč	As above	No

CLIMATE CHANGE & TRAVEL

Travel – especially air travel – is a significant contributor to global climate change. At Lonely Planet, we believe that all who travel have a responsibility to limit their personal impact. As a result, we have teamed with Rough Guides and other concerned industry partners to support Climate Care, which allows people to offset the greenhouse gases they are responsible for with contributions to energy-saving projects and other climate-friendly initiatives in the developing world. Lonely Planet offsets all staff and author travel.

For more information, turn to the responsible travel pages on www.lonelyplanet .com. For details on offsetting your carbon emissions and a carbon calculator, go to www .climatecare.org.

line C (red) runs from Háje in the southeast to Ládví in the north (extending north to Střížkov, Prosek and Letňany in 2008).

Line A intersects line C at Muzeum, line B intersects line C at Florenc and line A intersects line B at Můstek.

Services are fast and frequent. You'll find a map in every metro station and metro train, as well as on the pull-out map at the back of this book. In this book the nearest metro station is noted after the **M** in each listing.

TRAM & BUS

Regular tram and bus services (see www.dpp.cz for maps and timetables) run from 5am to midnight. After this, night trams (51 to 58) and buses (501 to 512) still rumble across the city about every 40 minutes. Night trams intersect at Lazarská in Nové Město. If you're planning a late evening, find out if one of these services passes near where you're staying.

Be aware that few tram or bus stops sell tickets. So if you're using single tickets, save a couple unstamped in your bag or pocket and validate them upon boarding.

GREENER WAYS TO PRAGUE

Catch a train to Prague and you might even discover one of Europe's best-kept secrets. Lined with sandstone bluffs and rocky outcrops that wouldn't be out of place in Arizona, the area on the German–Czech border – known respectively as Saxon or Bohemian Switzerland – makes for an atmospheric entrance into Prague as you travel down from Berlin. That's especially true if you hit the area at Děčín just before dusk.

Indeed, given the adventure and romance of rail travel, it's really not too much of a stretch to reach Prague by train all the way from London. See www.seat61.com for details.

RECOMMENDED MODES OF TRANSPORT

	Castle	Charles Bridge	Wallenstein Garden	Old Town Square	Wenceslas Square
Castle	n/a	Walk 10min	Walk 15min	Walk 15min, metro 1min, walk 3min	Walk 15min, metro 3min
Charles Bridge	Walk 10min	n/a	Walk 10-15min	Walk 10min	Walk 15-20min
Wallenstein Garden	Walk 15min	Walk 10-15min	n/a	Metro 2min, walk 3min	Metro 3min
Old Town Square	Walk 15min, metro 1min, walk 3min	Walk 10min	Metro 2min, walk 3min	n/a	Walk 5min
Wenceslas Square	Walk 15min, metro 3min	Walk 15-20min	Metro 3min	Walk 5min	n/a

TAXI

For years, Prague's taxi drivers have been renowned for scams and dishonesty. However, huge fines and crackdowns do seem to have made a difference recently. Most drivers now turn on their meters when picking up a fare, as legally required. If a driver doesn't, ask them to or get out and find a driver who will.

All this said, the taxi stands around Wenceslas Sq, Národní třída, Na příkopě, Praha hlavní nádraží, Old Town Sq and Malostranské náměstí are the most notorious rip-off spots. Hailing a taxi on the street – at least in a tourist zone – still holds the risk of an inflated fare.

Any trip within the city centre – say, from Wenceslas Sq to Malá Strana – should cost around 110Kč to 170Kč. A trip to the suburbs shouldn't exceed 300Kč, and to the airport 450Kč.

The best option of all is to call a reliable and honest radio-taxi service. In our experience, these include the following:
AAA Radio Taxi (☎ 14 014, 222 333 222; www.aaataxi.cz)
Halo Taxi (☎ 244 114 411)
ProfiTaxi (☎ 844 700 800)

PRACTICALITIES
BUSINESS HOURS

Banks 8am to 4.30pm Monday to Friday
Central tourist shops 8.30am to 8pm Monday to Friday, 8.30am to 6pm Saturday and Sunday
Department stores 8.30am to 8pm Monday to Friday, 8.30am to 6pm Saturday
Local shops 8.30am to 5pm or 6pm Monday to Friday, 8.30am to noon or 1pm Saturday

Main post office (Map pp98-9, E2; Jindřišská 14, Nové Město) 2am to midnight daily
Other post offices (www.ceskaposta.cz) 9.30am to 5pm Monday to Friday, 9am to noon Saturday
Restaurants 10am to 11pm

DISCOUNTS

A four-day **Prague Card** (www.prague card.biz; adult/student 740/490Kč) does exist, but as it mainly includes entry to the castle and a range of secondary museums, it would only be worth buying in exceptional circumstances. Do the sums carefully, to see if it will provide a saving.

EMERGENCIES

Although Prague is as safe as any European capital, the huge influx of money to the city has spawned an epidemic of petty crime.
Ambulance (☎ 155)
EU-wide emergency hotline (☎ 112)
Fire (☎ 150)
Municipal Police (☎ 156)
State Police (☎ 158)

LOST OR STOLEN BELONGINGS

Pickpocketing is unfortunately rife, especially in high season around the main tourist attractions. Keep your valuables well out of reach, and be alert in crowds and on public transport.

The former 'Foreigners Police Station' system was abolished in 2006. Today if you're the victim of theft, simply find the nearest police station and ask to fill out a standard form for insurance purposes. In theory someone should speak English at the **Prague 1 police station** (Map pp98-9, D2; Jungmannovo náměstí 9; Ⓜ Můstek), but be aware the police don't exactly have a reputation for helpfulness. For passports, contact your embassy (see www.expats.cz for listings).

HOLIDAYS

Banks, offices, department stores and some shops will be closed on public holidays. Restaurants, museums and tourist attractions tend to stay open.
New Year's Day 1 January
Easter Monday March/April
Labour Day 1 May
Liberation Day 8 May
SS Cyril & Methodius Day 5 July
Jan Hus Day 6 July
Czech Statehood Day 28 September
Republic Day 28 October
Struggle for Freedom & Democracy Day 17 November
Christmas Eve (Generous Day) 24 December
Christmas Day 25 December
St Stephen's Day 26 December

INTERNET

You'll never have any trouble finding an internet café in Prague, although prices vary wildly between 2Kč per minute in some pricier tourist spots to 1Kč in more reasonable central venues and even 0.50Kč a minute slightly out of the centre. Wi-fi access is also widespread.

Useful websites:

Expats.cz (www.expats.cz) Events listings, phone directory and discussions.
Living Prague (www.livingprague.com) Tourist advice.
Mapy.cz (www.mapy.cz) Excellent interactive map.
Prague Post (www.praguepost.com) Local newspaper.
Prague TV (www.prague.tv) Events listings, restaurant reviews, articles and discussion forums.
Praguexperience.com (www.praguexperience.com) Some bar tips.

LANGUAGE
BASICS

Hello.	*Ahoj.*
Goodbye.	*Na shledanou.*
	(pron: nas hladanou)
How are you?	*Jak se máte?*
Fine. And you?	*Dobře. A vy?*
Excuse me.	*S dovolením.*
Yes.	*Ano.*
No.	*Ne.*
Thank you.	*Děkuji.*
You're welcome.	*Prosím.*
Do you speak English?	*Mluvíte anglicky?*
I don't understand.	*Nerozumím.*

EATING & DRINKING

That was delicious!	*To bylo lahodné!*
Cheers!	*Na zdraví!*
I'm a vegetarian.	*Jsem vegetarián/ vegetariánka.* (m/f)
I'll pay/we'll pay.	*Zaplatím/Zaplatíme*

See p154 for some local staples and specialities.

SHOPPING

How much is it?	*Kolik to stojí?*
That's too expensive.	*To je moc drahé.*

EMERGENCIES

I'm sick.	*Jsem nemocný/ nemocná.* (m/f)
Help!	*Pomoc!*
Call the police!	*Zavolejte policii!*
Call an ambulance!	*Zavolejte sanitku!*

DAYS & NUMBERS

today	*dnes*
tomorrow	*zítra*
yesterday	*včera*

0	*nula*
1	*jeden/jedna/jedno* (m/f/n)
2	*dva/dvě* (m/n/f)
3	*tři*
4	*čtyři*
5	*pět*
6	*šest*
7	*sedm*
8	*osm*
9	*devět*
10	*deset*
11	*jedenáct*
12	*dvanáct*
13	*třináct*
20	*dvacet*
21	*dvacet jedna*
22	*dvacet dva*
30	*třicet*
40	*čtyřicet*
50	*padesát*
60	*šedesát*

70	*sedmdesát*
80	*osmdesát*
90	*devadesát*
100	*sto*
1000	*tisíc*

MEDICAL

Emergency treatment and nonhospital first aid are free for all visitors to the Czech Republic. Citizens of EU countries can obtain a European Health Insurance Card (EHIC); this entitles you to free state-provided medical treatment in the Czech Republic. Non-EU citizens must pay for nonemergency hospital treatment, and at least some of the fee must be paid upfront. Everyone has to pay for prescribed medications.

District Clinic (Map pp98–9, D3; ☎ 224 946 982; Palackého 5; ☼ 24hr; Ⓜ Můstek) Pharmacy (*lékárna*).

European Dental Center (Map pp98–9, E3; ☎ 224 228 984; Václavské náměstí 33; ☼ 8.30am-8pm Mon-Fri, 9am-1pm Sat; Ⓜ Muzeum)

Lékařsky Dům Medical Center (Map p131, D2; ☎ 242 426 400; www.ld.cz; Janovského 48; ☼ 24hr telephone service; Ⓜ Nádraží Holešovice)

Na Homolce Hospital (☎ 257 271 111; www.homolka.cz; 5th fl, Foreign Pavilion, Roentgenova 2, Motol; ☒ 7, 9, 10, 58, 59 from Ⓜ Anděl) Prague's best hospital, with multilingual staff.

MONEY

The Czech crown (Koruna česká, or Kč), is divided into 100 hellers (*haléřů*, or h).

Keep small change handy for use in public toilets and tram-ticket machines, and try to keep some small-denomination notes for shops, cafés and bars.

Many private exchange booths in central Prague lure tourists with attractive-looking exchange rates, which they don't actually offer when buying crowns. These are the selling rates or only available when changing huge sums. Check the small print before parting with any money. Better yet, just take money out of your own bank account using the widespread ATMs (*bankomaty*). Credit cards are also widely accepted.

How much Prague costs depends principally on where you choose to eat, how much you drink and whether you take any organised tours, but bank on spending anywhere between €30 to €75 a day, on top of accommodation. Sample costs:

Bottled water (1.5L) 12Kč to 20Kč
Prague Post newspaper 50Kč
Beer (0.5L) at least 60Kč in tourist pubs, 25Kč in nontourist pubs
Pork & dumplings 80Kč to 120Kč
Tour of Municipal House 150Kč
Cinema ticket 90Kč to 170Kč

NEWSPAPERS & MAGAZINES

The *Prague Post* (www.praguepost .com) is the city's leading English-language publication; German speakers will find *Prager Zeitung* helpful. These are widely available from the many kiosks around Wenceslas Sq and Na příkopě, along with a wide range of international press.

ORGANISED TOURS

There are scores of these, but the following are particularly interesting.

City Bike (☎ 776 180 284; www.citybike-prague.com)

Paul's Tours (☎ 602 459 481; www.walkingtoursprague.com)

Prague Walks (☎ 222 322 309; www.praguewalks.com)

Additionally, a fun way of getting around Prague is in an old 1950s/1960s convertible Škoda car (around 950Kč); you can't ring or book these, but you'll find them congregating at the southern end of Pařížská or at the corner of Karlova and Husova. Note that many visitors do not rate Prague boat trips that highly.

SMOKING

This is a favourite Czech pastime. Since 2006 restaurants and bars have been required by law to provide a nonsmoking area, but only at peak times and not necessarily screened off from smoking areas. Smoking is banned on the metro, buses and trams, on metro platforms and at bus and tram stops,

where you may face a 1000Kč on-the-spot fine. Unfortunately the line between the bus/tram stop and the street is not well defined.

TELEPHONE

The Czech Republic uses GSM 900, compatible with mobile phones from the rest of Europe, Australia and New Zealand but not with North American GSM 1900 or totally different Japanese phones. Some North Americans, however, have dual-band GSM 1900/900 phones that do work here; check with your service provider.

If you need to make many local calls, buying a Czech SIM card is a good idea, especially as local call charges are so low.

COUNTRY & CITY CODES

The dialling code for the Czech Republic is 420, but there are no area codes inside the country. All phone numbers have nine digits, which must be always dialled whether calling next door or a distant town. All landline numbers in Prague begin with a 2; mobile numbers begin with a 6 or 7.

USEFUL PHONE NUMBERS

International Direct Dial Code (☎ 00)

International Operator (☎ 155)

Local Directory Inquiries (national/international ☎ 1180/1181)

TIPPING

It's normal in pubs, cafés and midrange restaurants to add 10% to 15% if service has been good. If your taxi driver is honest and turns on the meter then you should round up the fare at the end of your journey.

TOURIST INFORMATION

The **Prague Information Service** (PIS; ☎ 12 444, 221 714 444 in English & German; www.pis.cz) can help with last-minute accommodation and has good maps and detailed brochures. Its main office is next to the Astronomical Clock at **Old Town Hall** (Map pp72-3, C4; Staroměstské náměstí 5; ☼ 9am-7pm Mon-Fri, to 6pm Sat & Sun Apr-Oct, 9am-6pm Mon-Fri, to 5pm Sat & Sun Nov-Mar).

Other locations:
Praha hlavní nádraží (Map pp98–9, G3; ☼ 9am-7pm Mon-Fri, to 6pm Sat & Sun Apr-Oct, 9am-6pm Mon-Fri, to 5pm Sat & Sun Nov-Mar)
Malá Strana Bridge Tower (Map p55, E2; ☼ 10am-6pm Apr-Oct; Charles Bridge)
Rytířská 31 (Map pp72–3, D4; ☼ 9am-7pm Apr-Oct, 9am-6pm Nov-Mar)

TRAVELLERS WITH DISABILITIES

Full of cobbled, hilly streets, Prague isn't an easy destination for people with limited mobility, although wheelchair ramps are becoming more common, and a few train and metro stations have self-operating lifts (see www.dpp.cz for more).

The **Prague Wheelchair Users Organisation** (☎ 224 827 210; www.pov.cz in Czech) can help with information and transportation.

Hotel Tuja (Kosicka 18
+ 420 603 527 685)

Saturday / sabado 22/03/08
- Wenceslas square / national museum
- Astronomical clock
- Charles IV bridge
  lunch at Hotel U hine
              (1.322 CZK)

- Letenske park
- Parijka (strut)
- Wine at monarch (2 glasses
  ⑤ NA PERSTYNE (strut)   100 CZ
- dinner at U MEDVIDKU (500 c
Sunday 23/03/08 - Prague castle
(tram 22) / lunch at old Tour
* square (hot dog + beer) + met
  back to St. Vitus cathedral,
  beer at U MEDVIDKU

✻ cafe nespresso

>INDEX

See also separate subindexes for See (p189), Shop (p191), Eat (p191), Drink (p192) and Play (p192).

000 map pages

INDEX

000 map pages